Configurations of Time

Imagining Other Temporalities in the Artist Residency

CONFIGURATIONS OF TIME

Angela Serino

SET MARGINS' #41

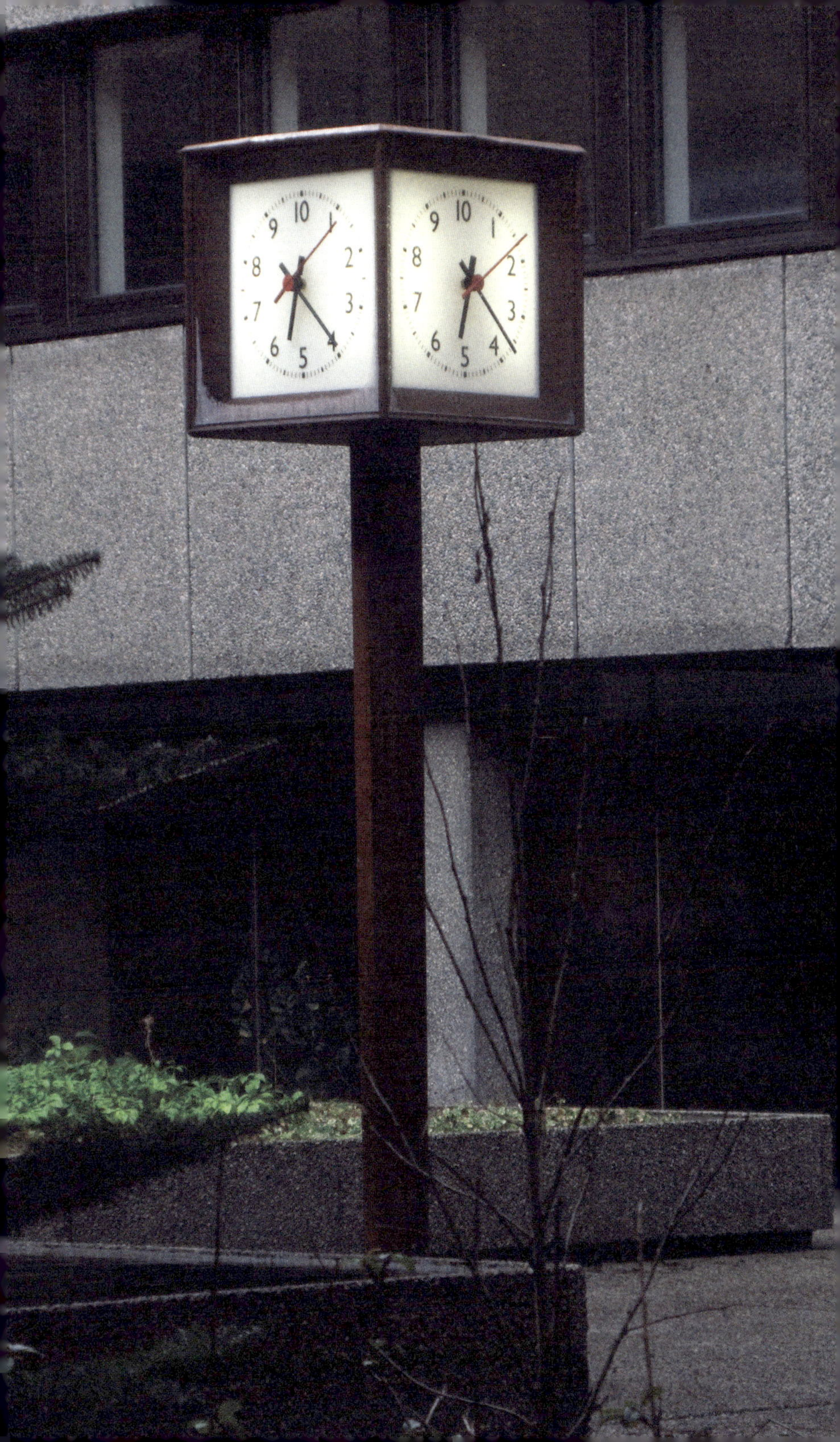
10 1 2 3 4 5 6 7 8 9
10 1 2 3 4 5 6 7 8 9

Toril Johannessen
HISTORICAL TIME (2011) — decimal clock, permanent installation at the University of Bergen.
Courtesy of the artist

CONFIGURATIONS OF TIME

This essay revolves around a collection of observations on

time

and

artist residencies

that I've put together in the past years.

By looking at different ways of thinking about and defining time, I will speak in terms of:

Astrophysics (or Space time)
Care time
Soil time

Space Time

Care Time

Soil Time

and the relation of these terms to residencies.

Each of the three sections ends with a set of questions which reflect the ambition to rethink the current model of artist residencies.

My interest in time comes from a map designed in 2015 by the Netherlands-based artist Marianna Maruyama in response to *Residencies as Learning Environments*, the international meeting of artistic residencies I curated together with FARE, the Italian Network of Residencies, in Milan. At that conference, I proposed to look at the residency as a learning situation that entails processes of individual or collective transformation — an experience that deeply affects the life and work of the resident artist, as well as that of those who enter in contact with her, like staff members, volunteers, other residency participants, and the various publics.

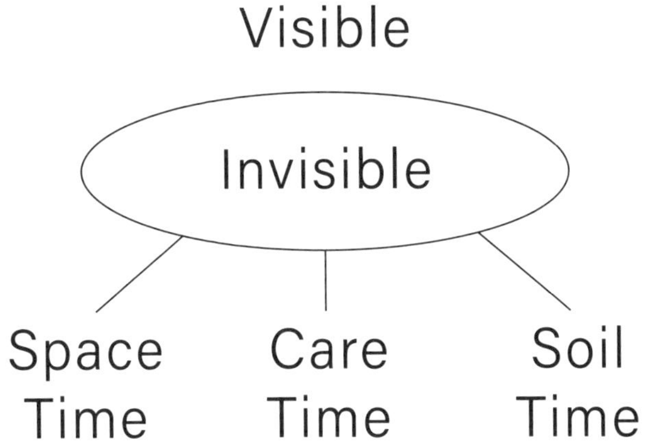

Several interesting remarks emerged from this two-day conference, which are highlighted in this map. In particular, by looking at residencies as open processes, what emerged was the existence of a tension between what is visible and what stays invisible whilst in residence.

ARTISTS' RESIDENCIES
SELF-DEFINITION
sense of permission
PROCESS
affirming
HEALTH
cultivating
bigger meaning of ecology
define sustainability
learn how to practice
keep living together after the residency has (officially) ended
triggers critical thinking
soft results
avoid romanticizing the local
teacher-in-residence
research-based, theory-based, practice-based
educational art project
society
art
education
radical pedagogy
needs
action
can we trace the long-term effect of our actions?
the imaginary
the visionary
a field of action
cross-pollination
learning
deferred value
courage to interpret
EDUCATION
LOCATION
ENVIRONMENT
agriculture
COMMUNITY DEVELOPMENT
strong
SOCIAL INCLUSION
CONNECT
CULTURAL PROGRAMMING
culture
CULTURAL HERITAGE
INTERNATIONAL DIALOGUE
THEME + FOCUS
exactly
what is being exchanged?
unquantifiable
production or education
education
temporary communities
gap between needs and institution
gap between and needs
TEMPORARY RETREATS
- remoteness
- liminal positions
- nature
(rural residencies)
to "withdraw"
- a temporary suspension
- a step aside to recharge/refocus and come back
communities that are INTENTIONAL and SPECIFIC ("affinities")
physical proximity (not only digital community)

work together
the imaginary, the
practice

in-residence
s' own academies
residency institution as a learning subject
public/participants as learning subjects

– scale
– discipline
to
textualize
– impact on communities
– reduce gap between regional and localized art practices
borders
DISPLACE OURSELVES – temporary (!) communities
possibility to fail
and develop
en process – tension – visible production – not always expecting tangible or specific things from artists
step-by-step
"deferred" value
cycles of visibility
TIME
How can we show more than one timeline?

hat could education be?
personal and collective
SELF-TRANSFORMATION
unframed KNOWLEDGE:
• no one method or technique
• no fixed curricula
• no verifiable/measurable with credits
• not only academic knowledge but embodied

he
eeds
institutions

RESIDENCY MODEL
EXPLODES
do
ts need?)
self-directed programs

Marianna Maruyama and Angela Serino
AiR RESEARCH MAP (2016) — drawing printed on paper.
Courtesy of the author and Marianna Maruyama

In the five years I worked as a member of the artistic committee of Kunsthuis SYB, a residency in Friesland, I struggled with the sense that the documentation of the time spent by guest artists in residencies — especially when the residency does not lead to an exhibition of finished works, but rather emphasises research time and exploration instead — is insufficient, or incomplete.

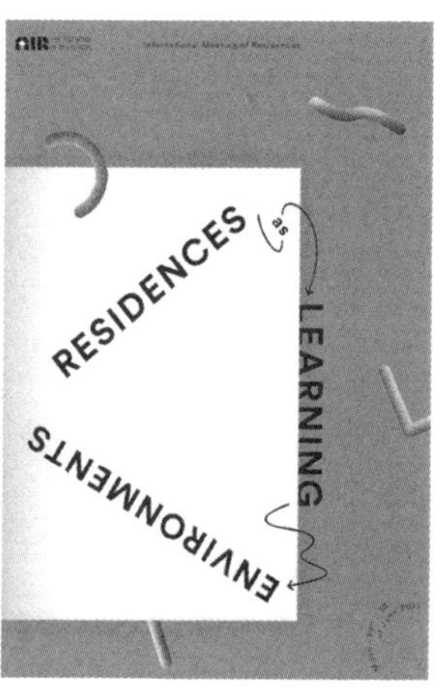

I also felt a certain ambiguity between what we would state we offered to artists — namely, the time and space to explore, fail, unlearn, and develop, often with no predefined end in mind — and the expectation (sometimes obligation) to directly show what the experience of hosting an artist brings to the residency as a site as well as to her practice.

Looking back at this map some time later during a working session at Kunsthuis SYB (2016), these thoughts took the shape of the following questions:

Can we have more than one timeline to describe a residency period?

If so, how can we represent it?

The expression "one timeline" refers to the common way of looking at residencies as singular, one-way timelines punctuated by consecutive events.

- the residency starts
- the residency is followed by a public presentation in the form of an event or open studio
- the residency ends
- a final report is submitted to the funding bodies

1 Founded in 2009 by Afterall, Chisenhale Gallery, Electra, Gasworks, LUX, Matt's Gallery, Mute Publishing, The Showroom, and Studio Voltaire, Common Practice is an advocacy group working towards the recognition and fostering of the small-scale contemporary visual arts sector in London. The report is: Sarah Thelwall, SIZE MATTERS: NOTES TOWARDS A BETTER UNDERSTANDING OF THE VALUE, OPERATION AND POTENTIAL OF SMALL VISUAL ARTS ORGANISATIONS (London: Common Practice, 2011). More info here: https://www.commonpractice.org.uk/research-papers/. Date accessed: September 6 2021.

I found confirmation of this sense of incompleteness echoed in the words of other curators and art critics at the time, particularly in concepts such as "deferred value" and "latency."

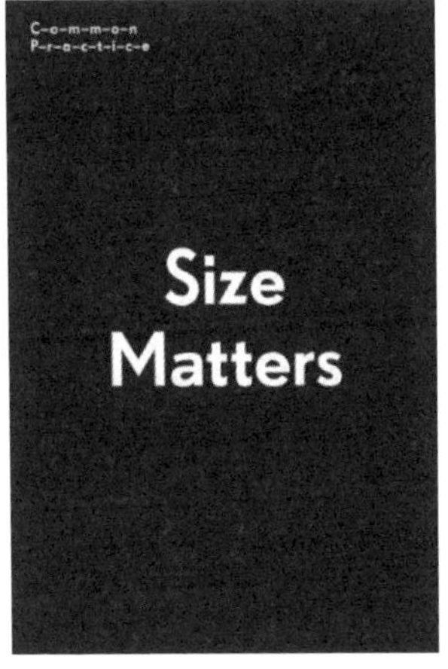

Taking inspiration from *Size Matters*, a report commissioned by the London-based network of small-sized art organisations Common Practice in 2011, curator and writer Nataša Petrešin-Bachelez identified similarities between this type of organisation and what happens at residencies.[1]

In both cases, these organisations often fail to keep track of the value of the artistic processes and works that they helped initiate, owing mostly to limited staff and funds.

'Deferred Value'

'Deferred value" describes a situation in which art organisations offer the conditions to start projects which will only be fully developed later on. As the value of the art projects develops throughout its lifetime, the initiating organisations are not the main beneficiaries, but often larger artistic and commercial institutions. 'When those organisations invest in an artist, the financial and social benefits of this investment rarely comes back to the organisation, and current formal reporting procedures are unable to capture this 'deferred value," whereby the value created by an initiating organisation is realised long after a commission has moved beyond its jurisdiction. I think that this particularity is also very often the case of residency programmes," Petrešin-Bachelez commented.[2]

2 Quote from a February 2013 email exchange between the author and Nataša Petrešin-Bachelez in which we discussed her article 'Reflexive Residency Structures" (2013), later printed in Alain Quireyns (ed.), AIR TRACES, (Antwerp: AIR Antwerpen 2013), 14 – 24.

3 Jan Verwoert, 'Exhaustion and Exuberance" in Vanessa Ohlraun (ed.), TELL ME WHAT YOU WANT, WHAT YOU REALLY REALLY WANT, (Berlin: Piet Zwart Institute and Sternberg Press, 2010), 32.

'Latency'

In questioning the idea of a singular timeline, I found art critic Jan Verwoert's praise of latency equally powerful. In his essay *Exuberance and Exhaustion* (2008), Verwoert speaks of latency to address the existence of a value that is not yet there, that remains hidden, or at least does not manifest right away, as a way to go against the present logic of 24/7 production.

> "In a high-performance culture, the beginning and the end of each given task is defined with brutal clarity. All parameters are set by an outside demand, and the job must be performed as fast as possible to meet the pending deadline. In art, however, how to start and where to end are crucial questions that often defy a regimented notion of time."[3]

Intrigued by these observations, I asked Dutch artist Laura Wiedijk about her experiences on residencies and whether it was possible to think of the existence of more than one timeline. Her reply was *Yield* (2016), a gripping account of her eight-month residency at WIELS, the contemporary art centre in Brussels.[4]

4 The lecture performance YIELD was developed in 2016. It was presented for the first time at the launch of RESIDENCIES AS LEARNING ENVIRONMENTS (2016) at M4gastatelier, Amsterdam, again at the Rietveld Academy (2016), and in 2019 at OT301 for the launch event of Kunstlicht Issue: 'Unpacking Residencies."

You can watch the live recording of YIELD performed at OT301 in January 2019, here: https://youtu.be/swrsozR37wg?si=_VKHhTeuJ0kCD2Tm. Date accessed 6 July 2021.

Yield opened with this image:

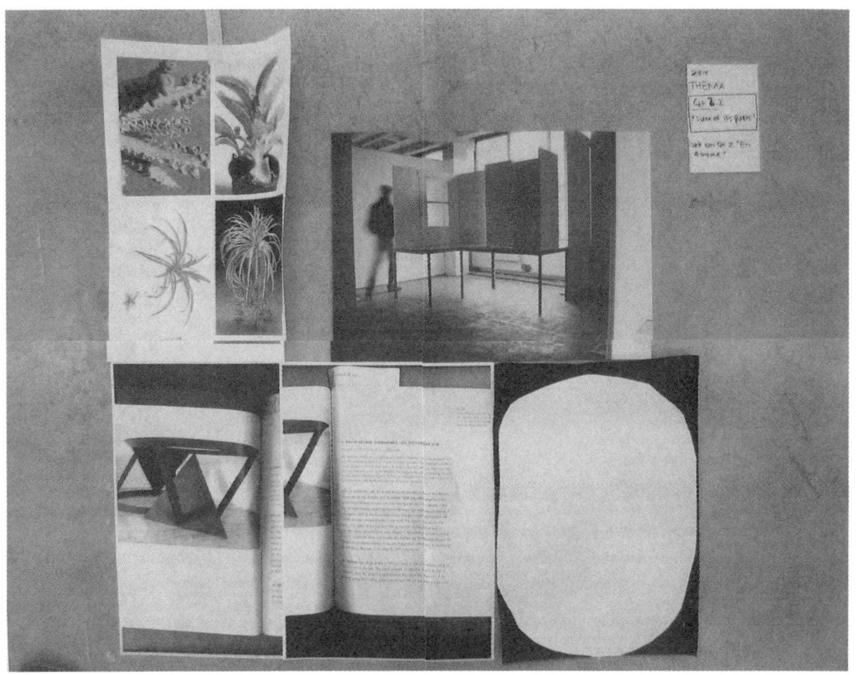

the unexpected result of a printing experiment gone wrong.

Laura Wiedijk
YIELD (2016) — video still.
Courtesy of the artist

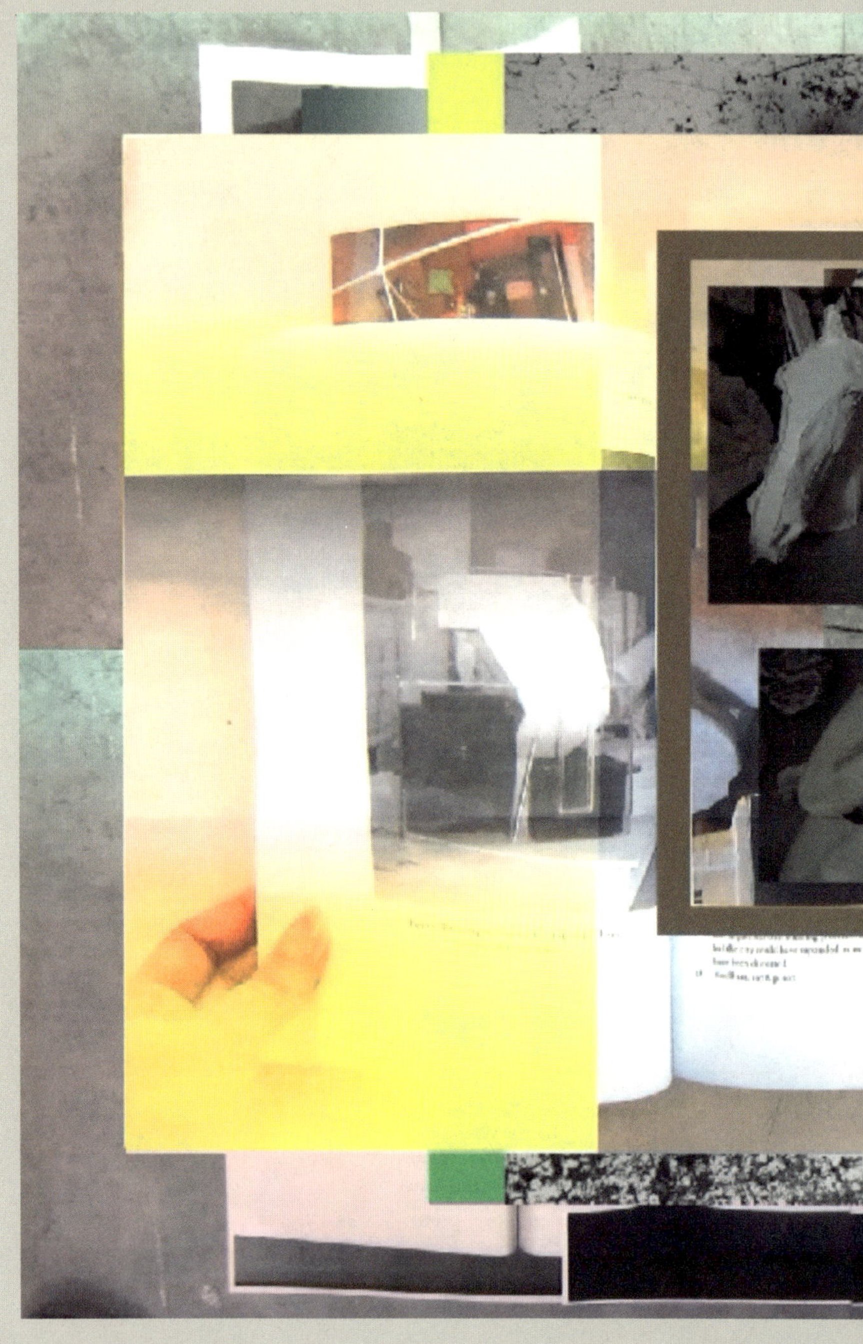

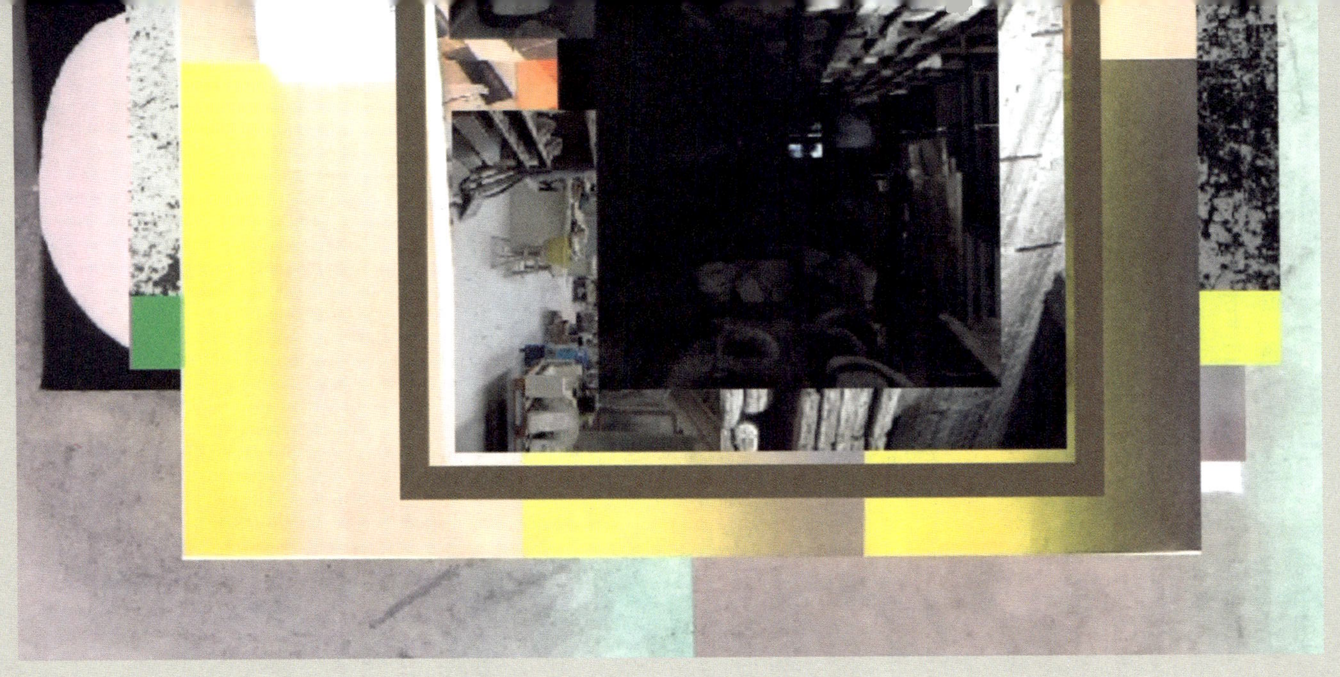

Laura Wiedijk
YIELD (2016) — video still.
Courtsey of the artist

During her talk, this colourful geometric print became a junction, a point at which various timelines would depart, each leading to different bodies of work developed later — after she had left the residency. Screens opened and closed into one another, like flowers blooming in time-lapse. Each series showed a different set of images: colourful and black-white pictures of working tables with assemblages in progress, corners of studio rooms, details of books or compositions photographed while they were tested. The various sequences were displayed at diverse speeds and rhythms, moving continuously in various directions, "with parallels, crossings and forks, ghosts and recurring melodies."[5]

As they developed, the public learned of the artist's work, potentially defined as an exploratory research on the gradients of colour, a future attempt to write with images, and a series of drawings of the "devil's spine" plants meant as studies for possible monumental outdoor sculptures. Some of these works were coeval, others followed one another over a period of about two years. Contrary to the idea of "a regimented notion of time," which emphasises productivity and immediate, tangible results, the artist showed that which had grown organically starting from that time spent reading, testing, and investigating in the studio at WIELS.

5 All quotations attributed to Laura Wiedijk are transcribed from YIELD (2016).

Yield ended with a provocative note to accept the impossibility of mapping the actual value of a residency as a statement:

> "The complexity of being in a residency makes reduction inevitable. The dailiness deems a lot as not worth mentioning. And even if the simultaneous lines of development of a residency can probably be represented, the simple documents are rarely accurate and the complex ones become unusable, swollen and unreadable."

When I look for Laura's residency at WIELS, the traces available online do not do justice to the richness of the tale presented by the artist.

To my eyes, Laura's work proved to me that how we speak and conceive of time spent in-residence—not just how it is registered formally—is fundamental and can open up new possibilities to define and discuss the value of a residency.

6 Angela Serino, "Cultivating Time," in Niko Doulos and Herbert Ploegman (eds.), UNPACKING RESIDENCIES: SITUATING THE PRODUCTION OF CULTURAL RELATIONS, Kunstlicht Vol. 39, n.2 (2018), 60 – 73.

In 2018, I wrote an article for a dedicated issue on residencies for the academic journal *Kunstlicht* where I introduced the expression of “thinking through time” as a possible approach to address this condition.[6]

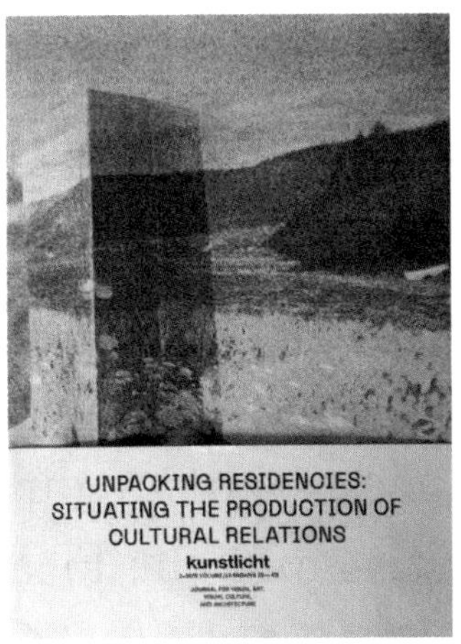

With this concept, I aimed to propose a way of discussing and engaging in residencies that acknowledges the various degrees of visibility affecting the resident's work. It involves considering different timelines, both when we as residency operators conceive our programmes, and when we respond to the administrators, private patrons, or public funding bodies that support them.

Could we possibly move on from thinking about the time of a residency as directly correspondent to the duration of the residency period?

Could we have different ways and tools to measure the value and the impact of the residency on the work of the artist and the location of the residency?

Could this new approach be sustained by the current economic system supporting us?

Space Time

One reading which helped me question the prevailing narrative of a pressured time, constrained and measured as a continuum of growing production, was

"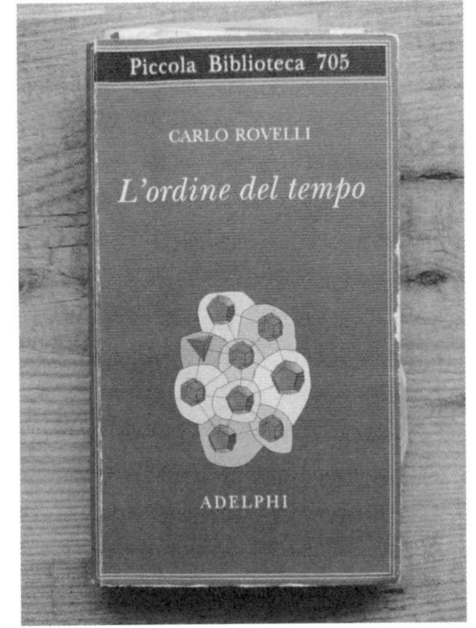"

Carlo Rovelli
THE ORDER OF TIME (2018)

by Italian theoretical physicist Carlo Rovelli.

Here, Rovelli reminds us that since Albert Einstein's theory of relativity, we know that there is no one single time.

"The single quantity 'time' melts into
a spider web of times,"

Rovelli states.[7]

7 Carlo Rovelli, THE ORDER OF TIME (New York: Riverhead Books, 2018), 15.

Time is not the same even if we use the same tool, for instance, a wristwatch: a watch that is on a table will go faster than the same watch that is on the floor.

This is a direct effect of the closeness to the Earth that, as Einstein explained, deforms space and time.

Louise Bourgeois
THE INSOMNIA DRAWINGS (1994 – 1995) — ink and pencil on music paper, 30.5 × 22 cm.
(Photo: Christopher Burke) © The Easton Foundation

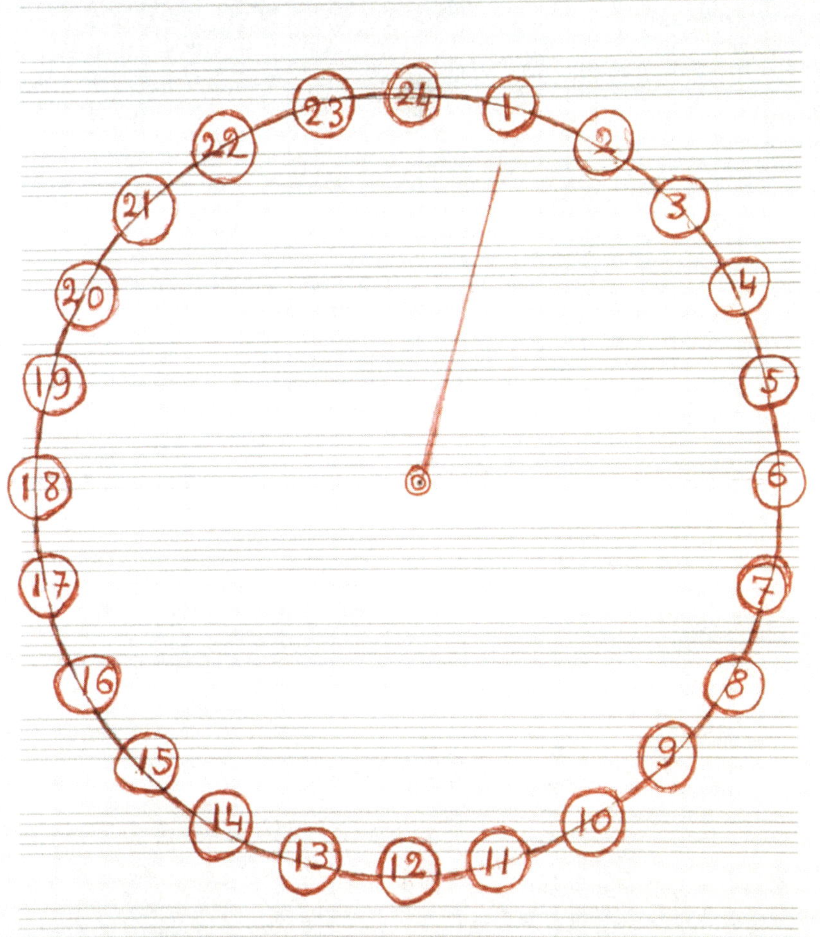

MANUSCRIPT PAPER

National Brand

LB

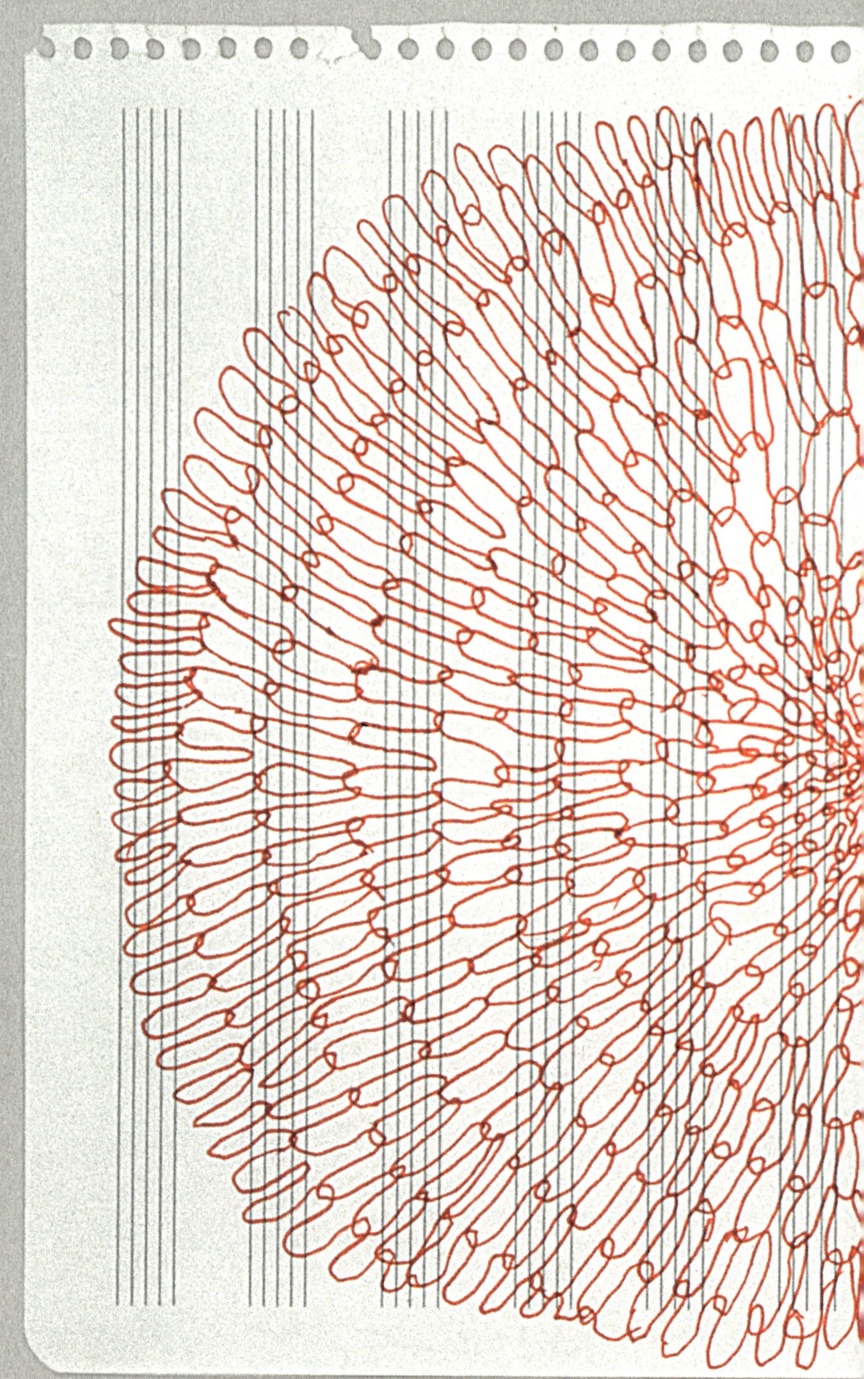

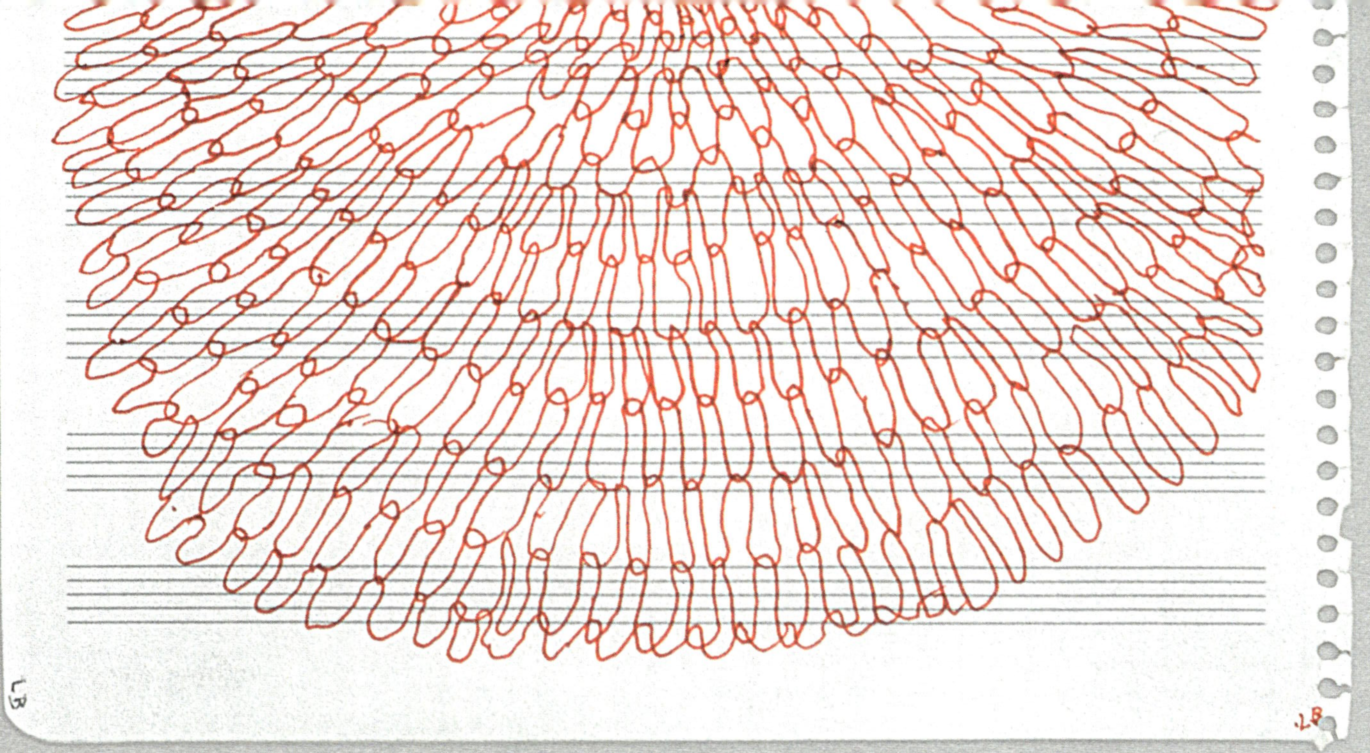

Louise Bourgeois
THE INSOMNIA DRAWINGS (1994 – 1995) — ink and pencil on music paper, 30.5 × 22 cm.
(Photo: Christopher Burke) © The Easton Foundation

Louise Bourgeois
THE INSOMNIA DRAWINGS (1994 – 1995) — ink and pencil on music paper, 30.5 × 22 cm.
(Photo: Christopher Burke)

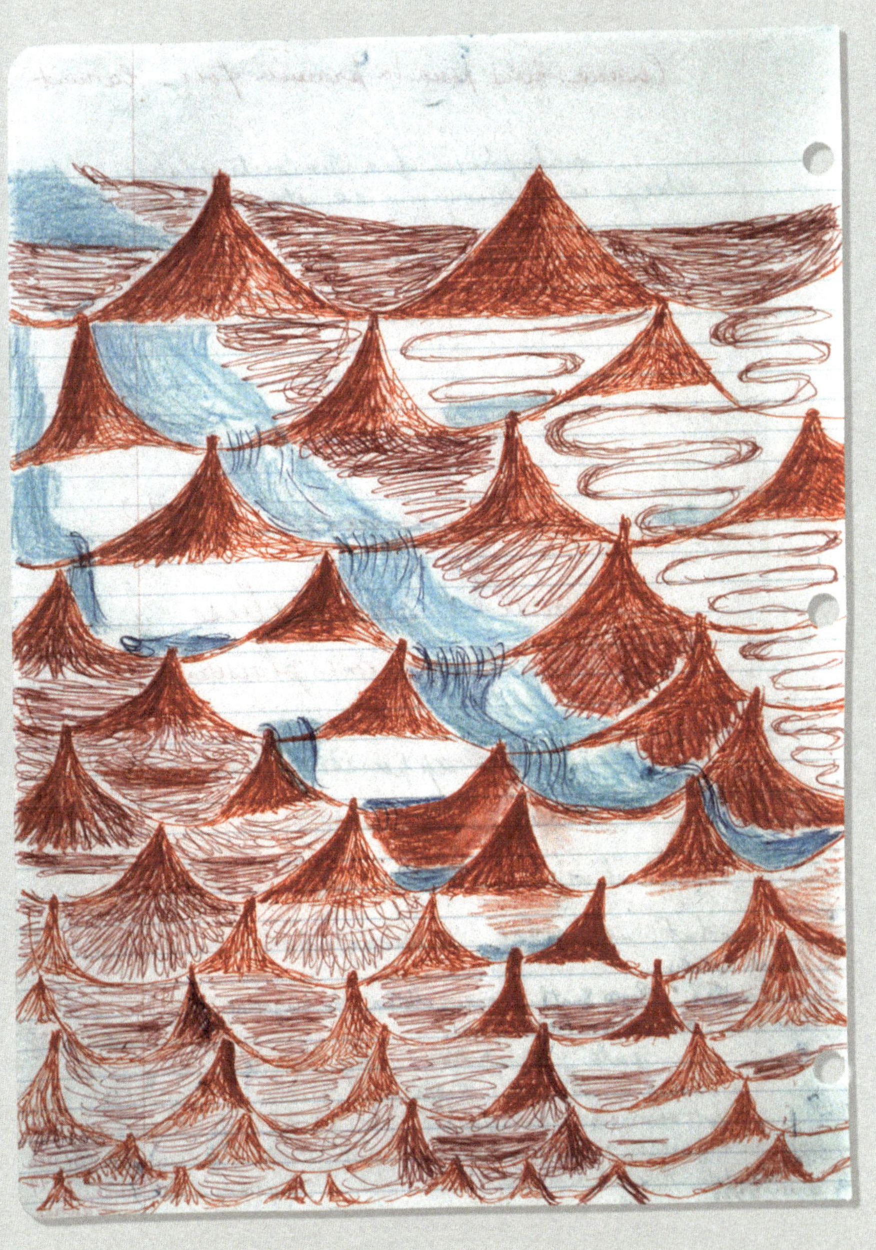

The following drawings are used by Rovelli to show that a common present does not exist.

1.

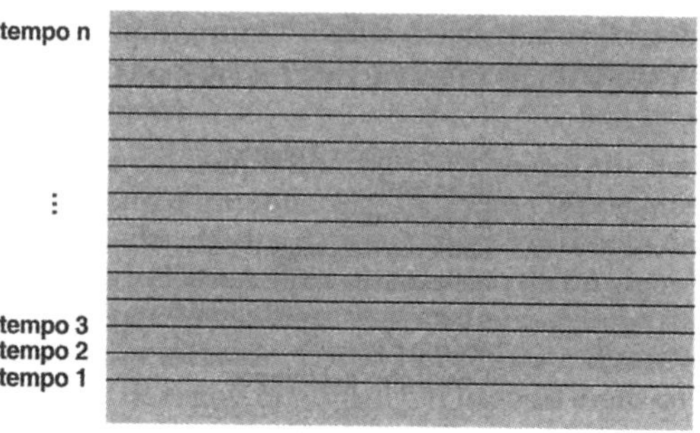

2.

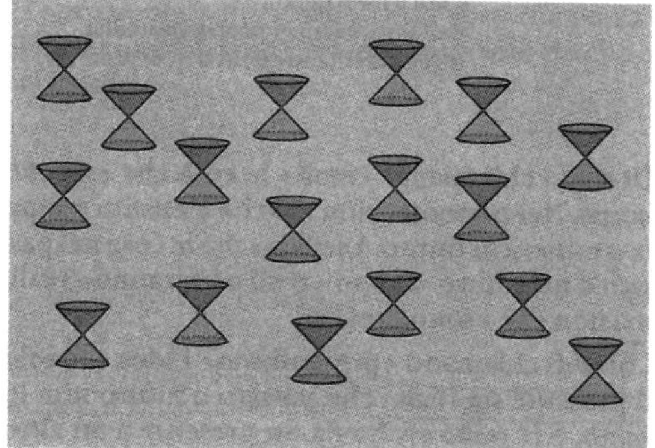

The temporal structure is not something like the drawing in Fig.1. This is how we conceived of time before Einstein. The second and third drawings better represent the actual temporal structure of the world. Space-time moves around and is itself not static.[8]

8 All drawings from Rovelli, THE ORDER OF TIME. Fig. 1, 2, Ibid., 94; Fig. 3, Ibid., 47; Fig. 4, Ibid., 109.

9 Ibid., 110.

In the world, according to quantum physics, we do not speak of time but of quantum space-time "that is fluctuating, probabilistic and discrete."[9]

3. 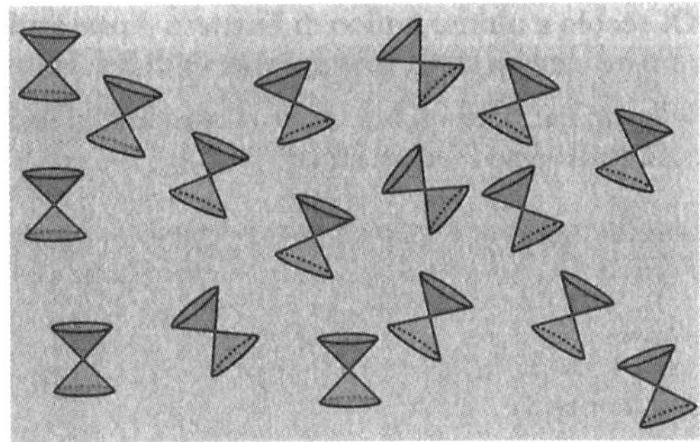

This figure is what Rovelli draws to show it.

4. 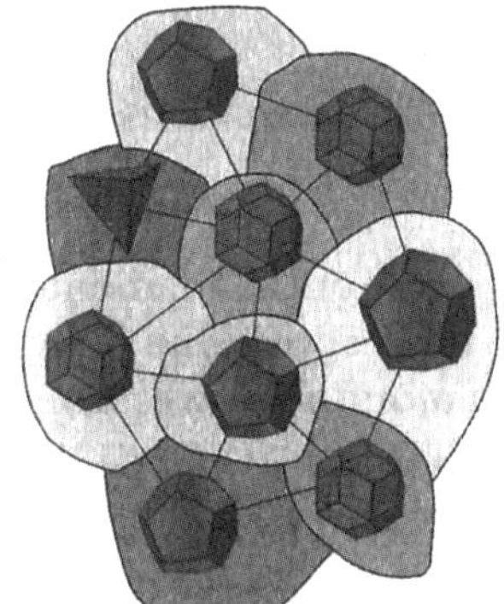

The various three-dimensional orthogonal shapes in this image are elementary grains or quanta of space.

Rovelli states:

> "These elementary grains do not exist immersed in space, rather they themselves form that space. They interact continuously with each other and they indeed exist only in terms of these incessant interactions. This interaction is the happening of the world, it is the minimum elementary form of time that is neither directional nor linear."[10]

This exercise in science tells us that an objective global present does not exist. The temporal structure of the world is more complex than a simple linear succession of instants. Space and time are events and relations.

10 Ibid., 108.

Moving out of an exclusive
now and present
means accepting that,
in a residency,
not all that I will have to say
has happened yet.

What we want to give
visibility to and at what
moment in time become
crucial questions.

Thinking along these lines, I would like to introduce "The Site Residency" as an example of a project that, by intentionally playing with the idea of artistic production, proposes a delayed restitution of a residency period, showing other possibilities of sharing the results of this experience with the public.

'The Site Residency" was developed by then-director Lívia Páldi and curator Sebastian Cichocki at BAC Baltic Art Centre, a residency organisation established in 2003 in Visby, a city on the island of Gotland in Sweden. Inspired by the land and conceptual art theories of the '60s and '70s, specifically their critique of the object status of an artwork, the residency challenged the idea of material production.

11 Lívia Páldi (ed.), THE SITE RESIDENCY (Berlin: BAC–Baltic Art Center and Sternberg Press, 2017), 9.

The three participating artists — Annika Erickson, Susanne Kreeman, and Agnieszka Polska — were invited to spend two weeks on the island between 2013 and 2015. On the cover of the publication produced two years after the residencies concluded, you can read the series of instructions written for the artists by Cichocki as an invitation to engage with the location of the residency place in different ways than they would usually work in their own studios, or in any other outdoor place where they were expected to produce something. The artists didn't have to propose any new work and were invited to "refrain from producing art on their regular terms for a while."[11]

After their stay, each artist worked with a ghostwriter who had never visited the site and relied on the traces of the place they collected during their residencies to write a fictional account, later published in the eponymous book.

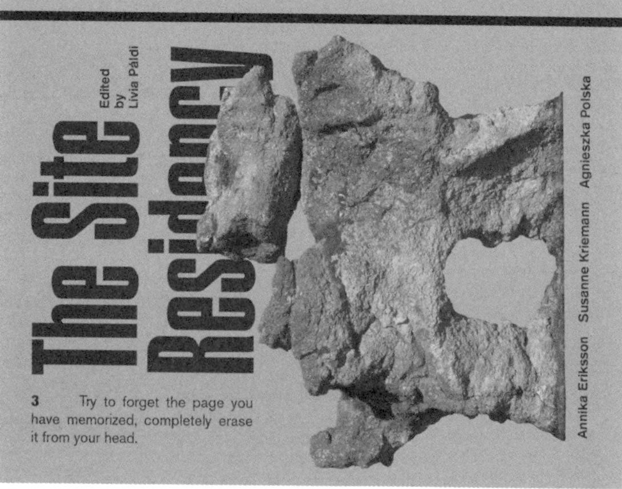

THE SITE RESIDENCY INSTRUCTIONS

Sebastian Cichocki

1 A moratorium on the Latin alphabet day: I'll refrain from reading and writing for twenty-four hours. I'll have no contact with books, magazines, notebooks, laptop screens, etc. I won't produce new written data for that day (please note that non-Latin alphabets are allowed).

2 Try to learn by heart a randomly chosen page from the book you have with you. Learn it while you're outside the house.

3 Try to forget the page you have memorized, completely erase it from your head.

THE SITE RESIDENCY GHOSTWRITING MANUAL

Sebastian Cichocki

I The text might be a novella, set of poems, novel, libretto, movie scenario, etc., but has to be fiction. There is no aim of producing a critical essay or to refer in any way to the artist's practice.

II The ghostwriter shouldn't visit the place where the artist has stayed.

The Site Residency

Edited by Livia Páldi

Annika Eriksson Susanne Kriemann Agnieszka Polska

4 Cycle to the place you have pointed to on the map with your eyes closed.

The Site Residency

5 Write some poetry today. You might want not to use words, but the objects found around you instead.

6 Create a garden patch with whatever stuff you may find lying around. Keep tending to it during the residency.

7 Find your walking path and retrace your steps each subsequent day.

8 Each day select one of the eight parts of speech—verbs, nouns, pronouns, adverbs, adjectives, prepositions, conjunctions, and interjections—and select ten words to describe your actual condition/situation.

BAC

SternbergPress

9783956793172

III The text should be delivered after no longer than ninety days.

IV If the artist wishes to somehow illustrate the text when it's finished, she/he can provide for this.

9 Keep repeating for several minutes a randomly chosen haphazard/occasional gesture or unintentional movement each day.

V The stay in Visby following the residency should be used for transferring the experience from the artist to the ghostwriter—talking, recording, taking notes, filming, etc.—and archiving the data for the writer.

Lívia Páldi (ed.)
THE SITE RESIDENCY (2017)
Design: Krzysztof Pyda

Those examples and ideas of time bring up
the following questions:

How many timelines can you draw looking at the works in your residency programme?

How many different tempos can you name within your programme?

What do you want to make visible from your residency work over time, let's say in 50 or 100 years from now?

What do you want to remain concealed for a specific duration, and why?

How would you define this time frame?

Would the artist-in-residence decide this, or the hosting institution?

How could you document the work of your residency and of the artist according to these different timelines?

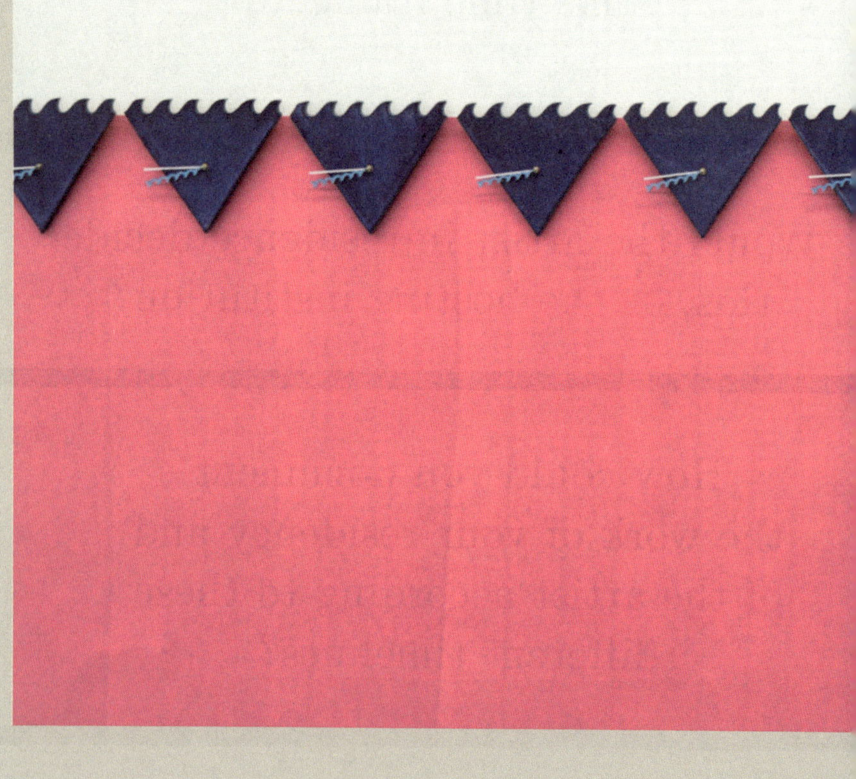

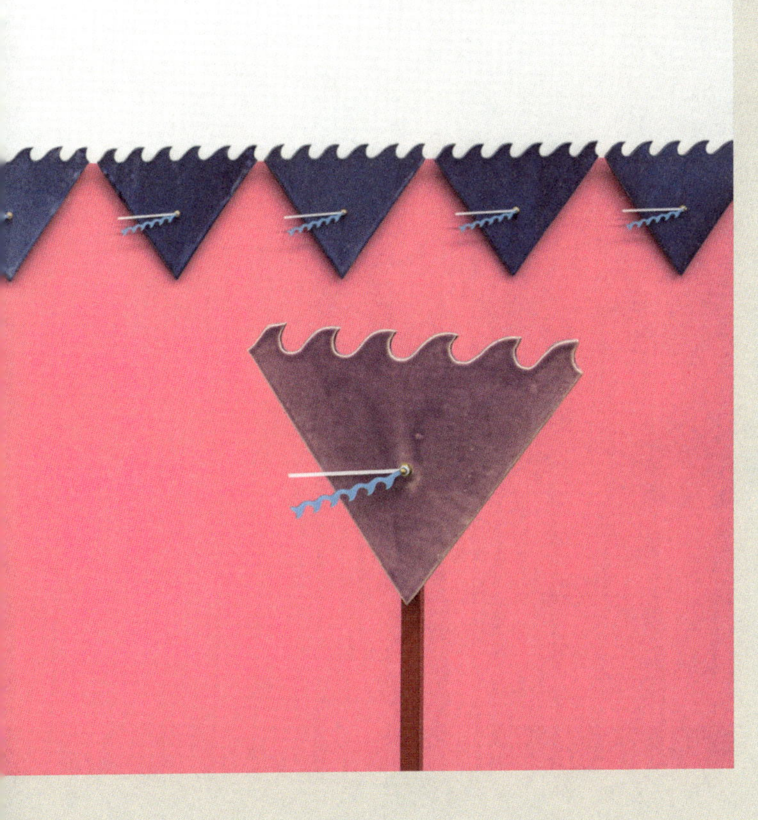

Every Ocean Hughes
BEYOND THE WILL TO MEASURE (2014) — ceramic clocks, variable dimensions up to 14 m.
(Photo: Doryun Kim) Courtesy of the artist

Care Time

12 Lisa Baraitser, ENDURING TIME
(London: Bloomsbury Academic, 2017), 13.

We move now to the second point of this essay.

An exploration of time where there is no event nor movement; where the impression is that nothing really happens. The reference for this idea of time comes from the work of British psychoanalyst and professor Lisa Baraitser, particularly her book

“ 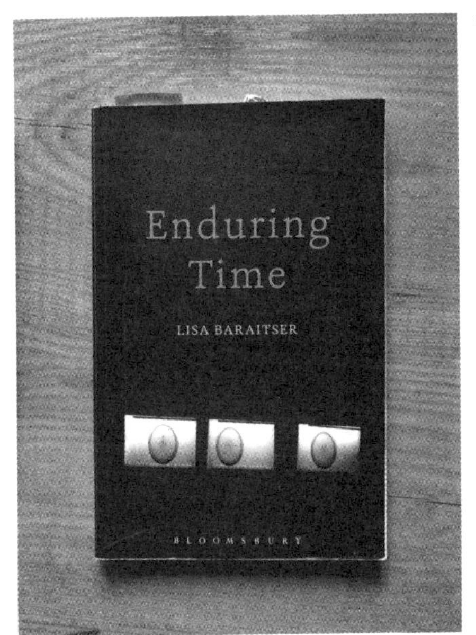 ”

Lisa Baraitser
ENDURING TIME (2017)

Drawing from an eclectic collection of material, Baraitser sets out to investigate a specific kind of time, one that "simply does not flow."[12]

Her work starts from noticing the existence of a prevailing narrative that insists on time as something stuck in between a traumatic past and the foreclosed future — what she defines as "non-stop inertia."[13]

Today we do not look forward to the future with hopes of positive changes and amelioration, a betterment of the now, as it was for instance after the Second World War in Western Europe. At the same time we have the impression that we live in a time that is always running up because it is frantic and hurried — symptomous of living in accelerated, late capitalist times.

> "In this temporal imaginary the present is experienced as time that is both relentlessly driven and yet refuses to flow."[14]

Non-stop inertia describes exactly this: the sensation of rushing towards something travelling at great speed, while at the same time feeling that one is not getting anywhere. Within this prevailing narrative, however, Baraitzer argues that

> "there are other types of time available for us that happen simultaneously in the condition of the now. The time that simply does not flow, that is suspended, is one of them."[15]

13 Ibid., 9.

14 Ibid.

15 Lisa Baraitser, "On Time, Care, and Not Moving On". 5 July 2018, ICI Berlin Institute for Cultural Inquiry. Available online at: https://www.ici-berlin.org/events/lisa-baraitser/ Date accessed: 1 March 2021.

What does suspended time mean in practice?

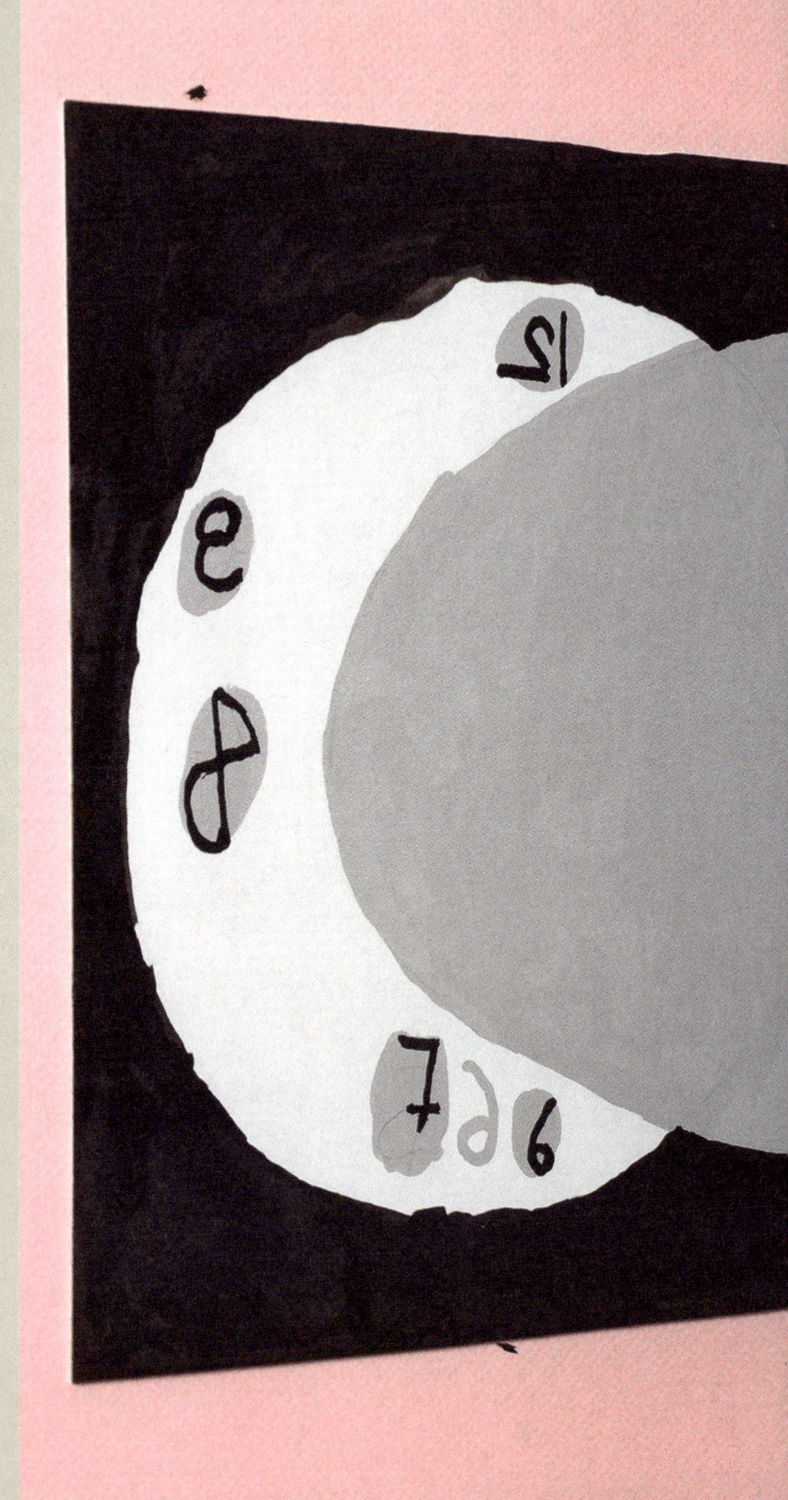

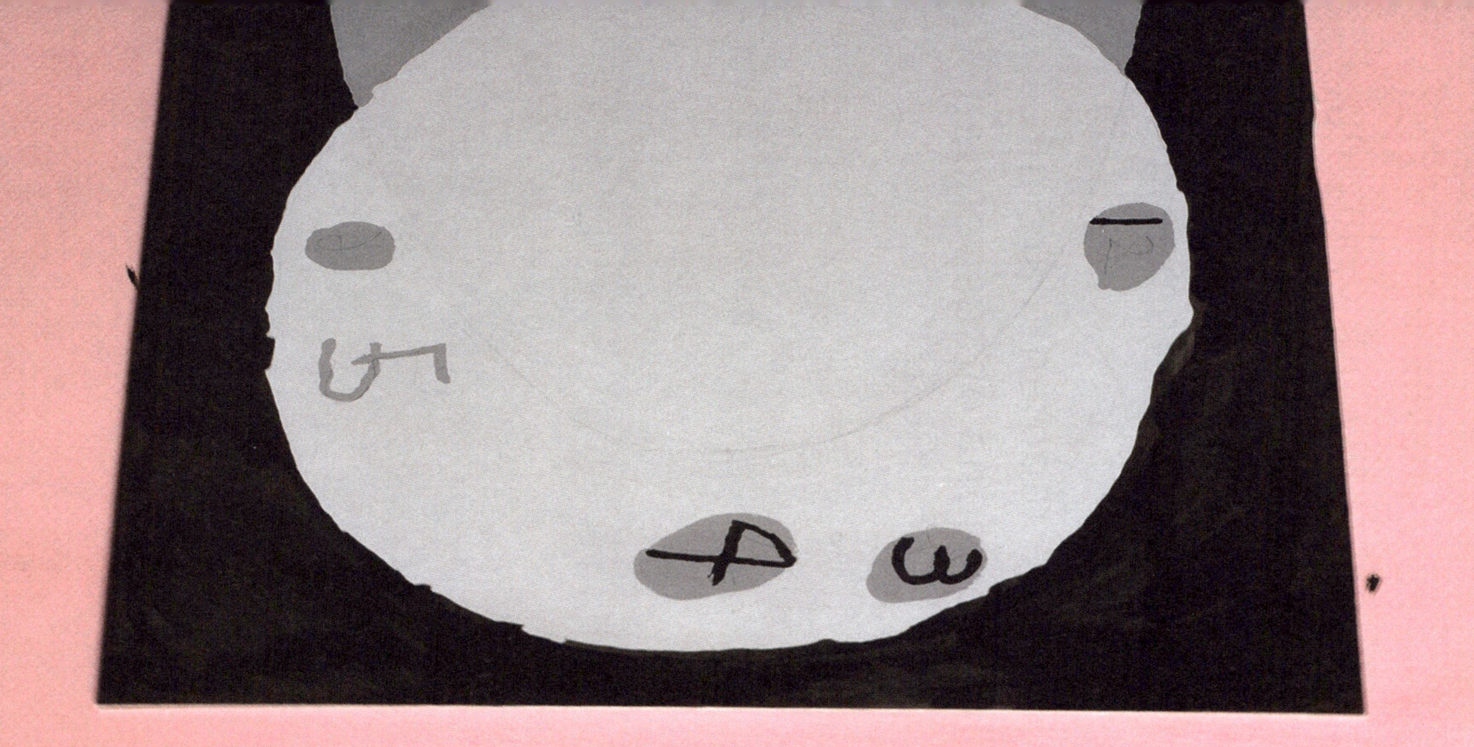

Katja Mater
TIME IS AN ARROW, ERROR 02 (2020) — two C-prints.
Courtesy of the artist and LambdaLambdaLambda Prishtina/Paris

Modes of
waiting, staying, delaying,
enduring, persisting,
repeating, maintaining,
preserving, and remaining –

these moments are all
expressions of suspended
time.

16 Ibid.

None of these modes have the allure of times which rupture, change, or shift. Rather, they involve social practices that are mostly arduous, boring, and mundane, "they are effectively dull moments."[16]

Yet, Baraitser argues, it is this kind of time that allows things to continue to exist. These are expressions of care that go on and on.

What is this care we speak about?

To elucidate this concept, Baraitzer discusses the work of other influential authors who have written about care ethics, including political theorist Joan Tronto and field philosopher Thom van Dooren. As they remind us, care has to do with the time that we live. It exists because we acknowledge that we each need another — that what we have in common is our interdependency and vulnerability. Yet, this is not a guarantee of a reality of an harmonious world.[17] Practising care for someone or something does not suppress challenges and conflicts. Baraitser reminds us that "ours is also a story of failures to care."[18]

Furthermore, it is to live "in a durational sense with affective states that touch also issues of gender, race, social injustice."[19]

17 Joan Tronto describes care as "a species activity that includes everything that we do to maintain, continue, and repair 'our' world so that we can live in it as well as possible" (1993). Baraitser, ENDURING TIME, 14; For Thom van Dooren: "... care is grounded in all of the 'inescapable troubles of interdependent existences', and can offer no guarantee of a 'smooth harmonious world'" (2014). Baraitser, ENDURING TIME, 15.

18 Baraitser, "On Time, Care, and Not Moving On".

19 Ibid.

20 This is even more visible in the current discussion about residency programmes. In the aftermath of the break caused by the Covid 19-pandemic, I have participated in several conversations stressing the urgency to redefine how we come together to work and live. In particular, the pandemic has accelerated the discussion about how these programmes can accommodate other temporalities of life: for example, of women/parent artists and of other able bodied individuals. See, for instance, the programme of the annual conference of Res Artis, the worldwide network of arts residencies. The 2023 conference, titled "Mind the Gap: Designing Residencies for Everyone," explicitly focused on issues of inclusivity and diversity (London, 6 – 9 September). This search for new principles and methodologies for institutional models that consider the needs of many is not exclusive to residencies, though. These same questions permeate the art field in general.

What can we do to cultivate *care time* in residencies?

When I think about this approach towards time, Baraitser's words raise questions about the sustainability of the work of residency staff and professionals — the fear of breaking down, of falling out or apart, and the tension between self-care and proper care of the artist in residence.

They also push us to check and discuss how our behaviour can reproduce inequalities and privileges inside our organisation. This concerns conditions of access and representation, working procedures and routines, and how these processes shape the identity of the residency. [20]

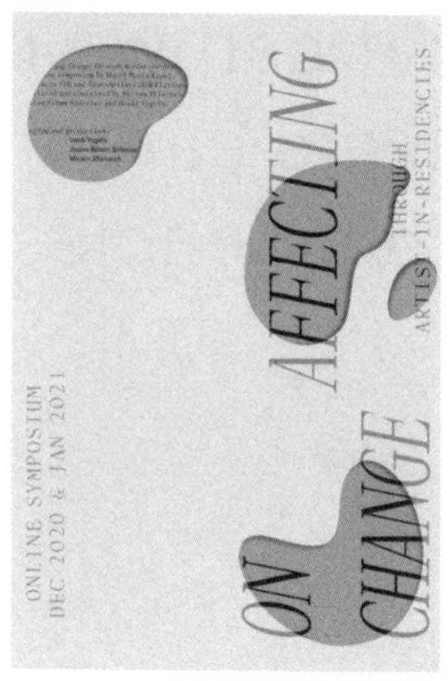

One possibility would be to develop one's own organisational tools for care and labour, as proposed by the Dutch residencies Hotel Maria Kapel, Kunsthuis SYB, and DutchCulture | TransArtists.

Drawing on several contributions proposed at the recent symposium "On Affecting Change Through Artist-In-Residencies," these three small-sized Dutch organisations recommend several useful working tools, ranging from complete and clear check-in and check-out procedures; shared documents which provide all relevant information regarding the position and politics of the institution; the opportunity to invite an external figure, a "shadow curator" who can offer reflections on and constructive alternatives to the curatorial process of the institution, thus promoting accountability and critical review; and more.[21]

21 The online symposium ON AFFECTING CHANGE THROUGH ARTIST-IN-RESIDENCIES took place between December 2020 and January 2021. It was organised by Hotel Maria Kapel, Kunsthuis SYB and TransArtists | AiR Platform NL. It was initiated and conceived by Miriam Wistreich, Josine Sibum Siderius and Heidi Vogels. You can find more information on the programme here: https://www.transartists.org/en/symposium-affecting-change-through-artist-residencies. Date accessed: 9 September 2021. A complete list with the description of the suggested "Tools for Care and Labour" are available here: https://www.transartists.org/sites/default/files/2021-07/On_Affecting_Change_online.pdf. Date accessed: 9 September 2021.

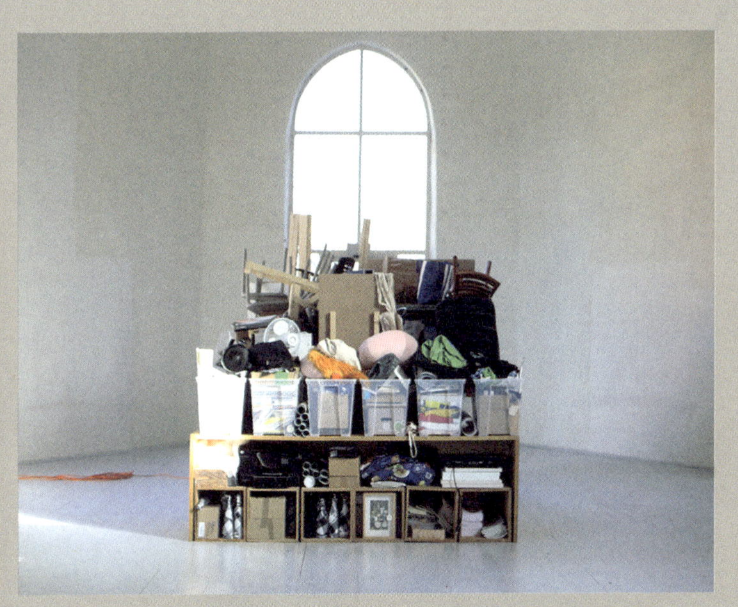

Maja Bekan, Griet Menschaert, Miriam Wistreich
SLOW BURN (2019) — space intervention.
Courtesy of Hotel Maria Kapel

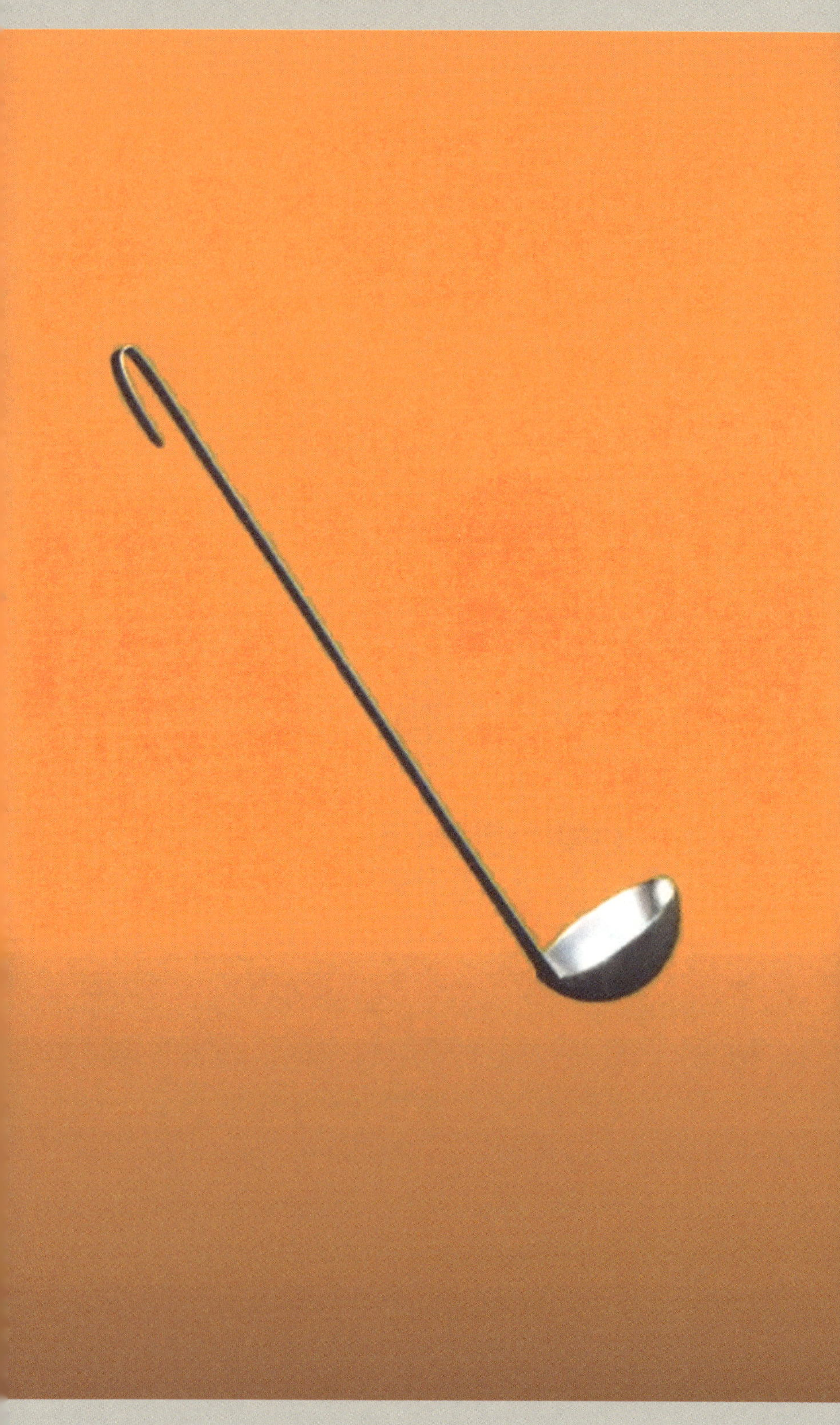

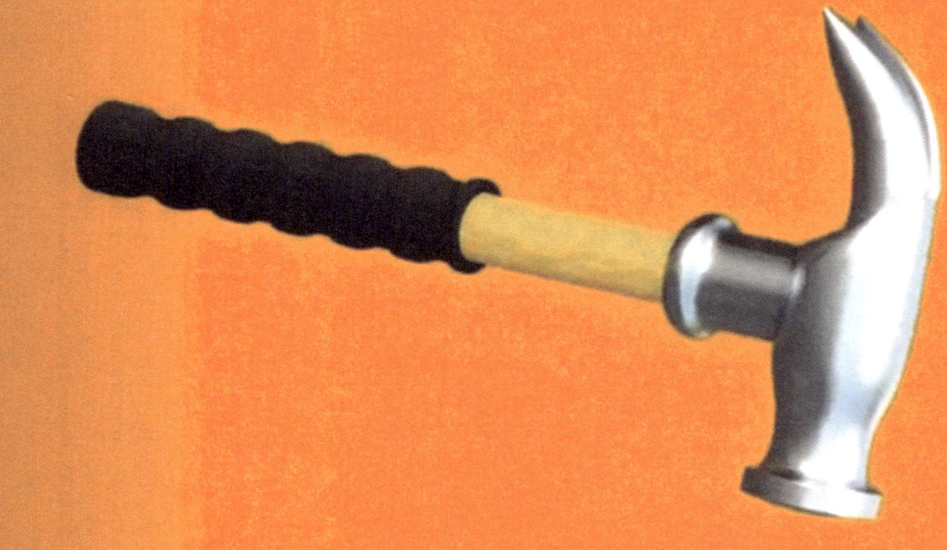

Harriet Rose Morley
TOOLS FOR COLLECTIVE NAVIGATION (2020) — still from screensaver rendered by Alex Paul Burch.
Courtesy of the artist and Alex Paul Burch

I'd like to present the example of another Dutch institution.

It is not an artist residency, however, its activity is significant to the point I am making here about *care time.*

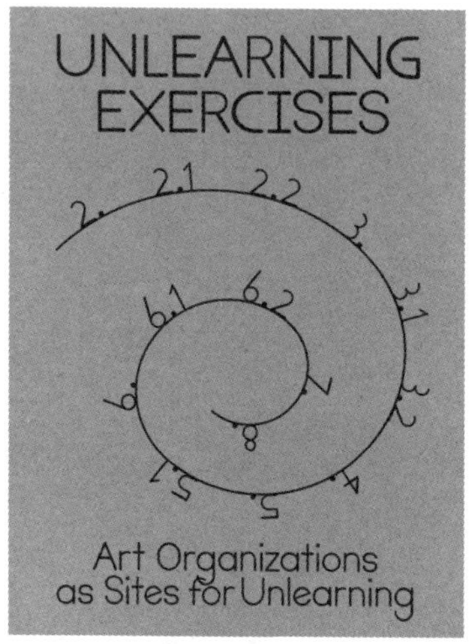

UNLEARNING EXERCISES:
ART ORGANIZATIONS AS SITES FOR UNLEARNING
Utrecht, The Netherlands: Casco Art Institute, Working for the Commons; Amsterdam: Valiz (2018)

EDITORS: Binna Choi, Annette Krauss, Yolande van der Heide, Liz Allan
CONTRIBUTORS: Liz Allan, Yollotl Alvarado, Antariksa, Jacob Apostol, Binna Choi, Joy Melanie Escani, Andrés García, Brigitta Isabella, Faisol Iskandor, Ismiatun, Nancy Jouwe, Annette Krauss, Emily Pethick, Andrea Phillips, Ying Que, Kerstin Stakemeier, Sakiko Sugawa, Syafiatudina, Ferdiansyah Thajib, Marina Vishmidt, Yolande van der Heide, Erminah Zaenah, and the shifting team at Casco Art Institute: Working for the Commons.
DESIGN: Rosen Eveleigh. Courtesy of the authors.

22 Binna Choi, Annette Krauss, Yolande van der Heide, Liz Allan (eds.), UNLEARNING EXERCISES: ART ORGANIZATIONS AS SITES FOR UNLEARNING, (Amsterdam: Valiz, Casco Art Institute, 2018), 149.

This institution is Casco Art Institute, in Utrecht.

In 2014, together with the artist Annette Krauss, the staff embarked in a series of 14 exercises over a period of more than four years, to unlearn the psychosomatic state of busyness — basically, how we embody the unnatural rhythm of being busy all the time.

One of the most structural exercises they did was spending two hours collectively cleaning the office every Monday, which has now become an institutional habit. This coll-ective action was the result of an internal staff discussion, where it became clear that being busy meant that actions such as cleaning, fixing and caring for the space — the "invisible" work — was always being pushed to the bottom of the to-do list, becoming the responsibility of a specific few staff members, like interns and volunteers.

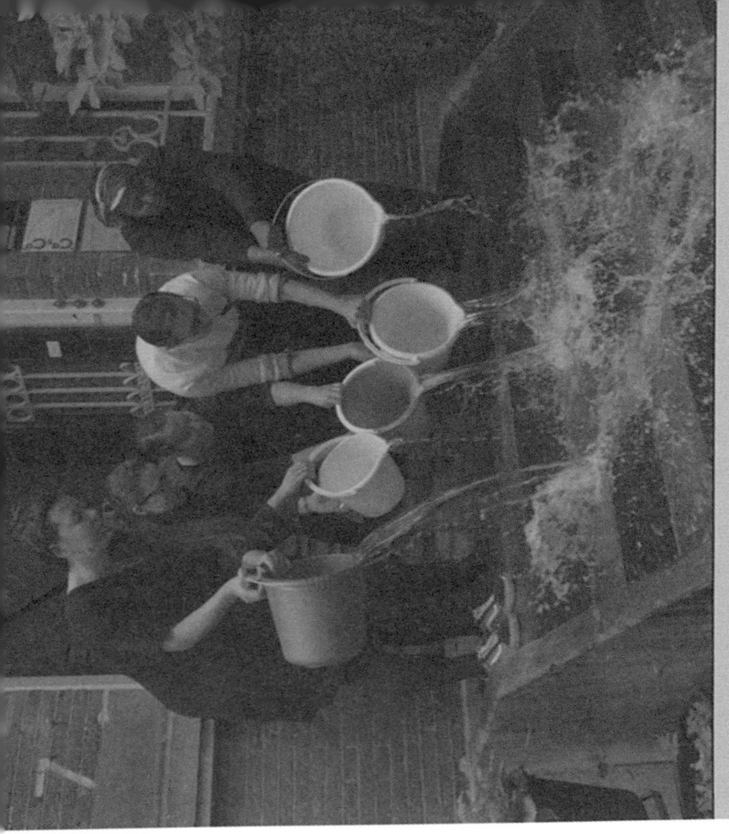

TOGETHER

UNLEARNING EXERCISE

We clean our office together every Monday morning after the team meeting. We divide the tasks, put on music (sometimes), and set the timer for around thirty minutes. It's important to begin cleaning together and feel we are collectively responsible.

WHAT TO UNLEARN

Undervaluing reproductive labor; hierarchies and unequal division of domestic labor in terms of who does what; and making reproductive labor the last priority and not finding any satisfaction in it.

Casco Team and Annette Krauss, "3. Cleaning Together (with Mierle)" (2014). As part of *Site for Unlearning (Art Organization)*. Photo: Annette Krauss

Yolande Zola Zoli van der Heide, one of the participants and former deputy director of Casco stated about this experience:

> ‘We now all clean together at the same time every Monday in a ‘minor’ effort to resist the capitalist conditioning that separates production from reproduction and devalues the latter, thus also discarding the bodies of colour that often take up this work, in order to sustain its mechanisms of influence and oppression.”[22]

What the Casco example shows is that actively creating occasions for conversation and open dialogues among all the people working in a residency or art institution is undoubtedly a key step towards checking what care we practise and for whom we care. This is also a precondition for possible changes.

UNLEARNING EXERCISES:
ART ORGANIZATIONS AS SITES FOR UNLEARNING
Utrecht, The Netherlands: Casco Art Institute, Working for the Commons; Amsterdam: Valiz (2018), 28 – 29. Images from the e-book.

2.1
OFF-BALANCING CHAIRS

2.2
ASSEMBLY

3.
CLEANING TOGETHER

3.1
DIGITAL CLEANING

3.2
REWRITING MAINTENANCE MANIFESTO

* How would we relate to each other, think, live and work with each other, if we started counting from two instead of one, not pretending that we know where and how things start, but that our selves are always already two, if not multiple...?

5.
CARE NETWORK

5.1
MOOD COLOR

6.
PROPERTY RELATIONS

6.1
WORK AND WELL-BEING

6.2
(COLLECTIVE) AUTHORSHIP

7.
TIME DIARY

8.
PASSION AND OBSTACLE

UNLEARNING EXERCISES:
ART ORGANIZATIONS AS SITES FOR UNLEARNING
Utrecht, The Netherlands: Casco Art Institute, Working for the Commons; Amsterdam: Valiz (2018), 20 – 21. Images from the e-book.

The questions emerging from this idea of time are:

When I speak about care time
in my residency,
whose time am I borrowing?
Or would I lend my own?

When I care,
for whom do I care?

How can we care together
with others?

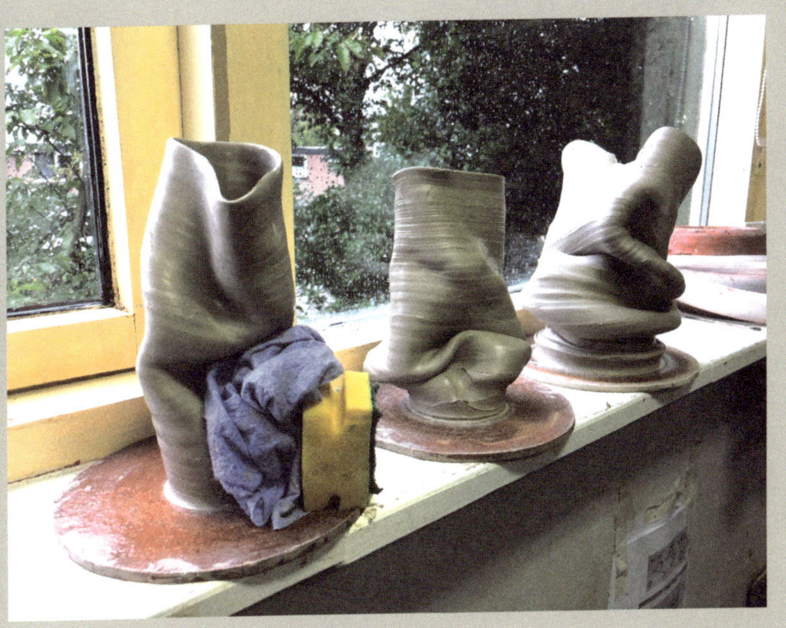

Tamara Kuselman
work–in–progress of A POOL WITHOUT A RIM (2020)
Courtesy of the artist

The conditions of care are not the same for everyone.

There are asymmetric conditions and unequal access.

What do our failures to care tell us?
Do we sit comfortably with them?

Did you fail to take care of yourself while taking care of your guests?

Can we think of a system
beyond reciprocity?
Is that generosity?

How do we create
networks of care?

How can you trace relations of interdependency — of your organisation, as well as your own relations in the workplace?

In conversation with:

Leonore Schruth
(Pupil)

Time:

Between the 1st and 2nd lockdowns

L: I have never heard of the term public time. Maybe public time is when I am in the city ... or in the tram ... or in public space.

J: And Corona public time?

L: It's when I'm wearing a mask ... or keeping distance.

Subject: PUBLIC TIME

www.school-of-temporalities.info

School of Temporalities (Maja Bekan, Annette Krauss, Julia Wieger)
HOW IS PUBLIC TIME? (2021) — posters.
Courtesy of the artists

In conversation with:

Sabine Bitter
(Artist / curator of this show)

Time:

Between the 1st and 2nd lockdowns

J: Are we together in this time? Are we experiencing the same time?

S: There were people who had to work and people who could not work.

A: Some people did not work so much, others worked more, others lost their jobs.

M: Are these people in the same time?

Subject: HOME / MIGRATION

www.school-of-temporalities.info

School of Temporalities (Maja Bekan, Annette Krauss, Julia Wieger)
HOW IS PUBLIC TIME? (2021) — posters.
Courtesy of the artists

In conversation with:

Alice Trost
(Radio host / kindergarten teacher)

Time:

Just before the 3rd lockdown

M: How much can you sustain not knowing about the future with Corona? I mean, how long can you keep up with this condition?

Al: I work with deadlines. I will try to survive till next spring, then I will fall apart.

Subject: UNKNOWN

www.school-of-temporalities.info

School of Temporalities (Maja Bekan, Annette Krauss, Julia Wieger)
HOW IS PUBLIC TIME? (2021) — posters.
Courtesy of the artists

Soil Time

23 María Puig de la Bellacasa, MATTERS OF CARE, SPECULATIVE ETHICS IN MORE THAN HUMAN WORLD (Minneapolis and London: University of Minnesota Press, 2017), 189. See in particular Chapter 5: 'Soil Times. The Pace of Ecological Care."

We arrive now to the third part
of this essay, inspired by soil.

What is soil and *soil time*?

Soil is the texture of the living world. Picture it as a skin that envelops the whole earth. It has a depth between 70 and 200 centimetres and nurtures plants and the animals that eat the plants.

Without life in the soil, life on our planet would not be possible.

In human geography, soil has been principally conceptualised as a resource, a natural thing belonging to the world of physical science. It is something that has always been there, and something from which we take. In reality, as several recent studies have shown, soil is both lively and alive, that is, it is composed of living and non-living components which have many interactions.

'Soil is not just a habitat or medium for plants and organisms; nor is it just decomposed material, the organic and mineral end product of organism activity. Organisms are soil. A lively soil can only exist with and through a multispecies of biota that *makes* it, that contributes to its creation."[23]

I first read about soil time in *Matters of Care* (2017) by María Puig de la Bellacasa, a writer and professor whose research occurs at the intersection of science and technology studies, feminist theory, and the environmental humanities.

“ 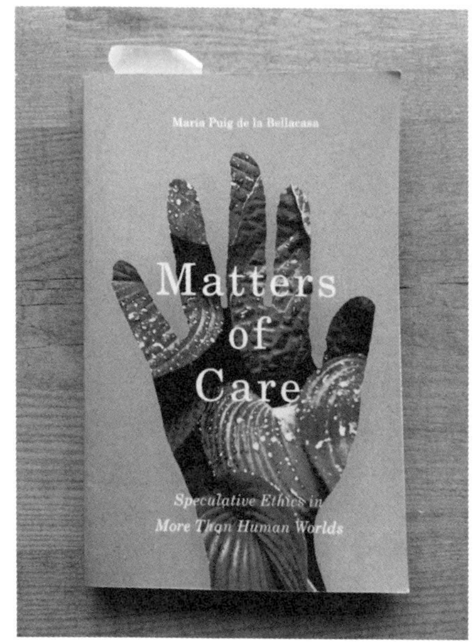 ”

María Puig de la Bellacasa
MATTERS OF CARE (2017)

In her book, Puig de la Bellacasa discusses permaculture and material spiritualities as forms of ecological care that challenge a seemingly "dominant mode of futurity in technoscience" that shape science, economy and agriculture, and their reductive notion of growth and innovation.[24]

24 Puig de la Bellacasa, MATTERS OF CARE, 174.
25 Ibid., 191.
26 Ibid., 176.

To speak of *soil time* is to speak of ethical relations with the more-than-human.

It is to become aware of the existence of different temporalities between biophysical entities and processes that make our soil alive.

> It means ceasing to ignore '"the complex diversity of soil-renewal processes in favour of linear temporalities aimed at speeding up abundant output,"

Puig de la Bellacasa writes.[25]

> 'Soil is created through a combination of the long, slow time of geological processes such as those taking thousands of years to break down rock — qualified as 'deep time' — and by relatively shorter ecological cycles by which organisms and plants, as well as humans growing food, decompose materials that contribute to renew topsoil. Both micro and macro timescales at stake in ecological relations involve different time-frames than those of human lifespan and history. This is not only a philosophical or scientific problem, it is an ethical and political one." [26]

To address soil time in relation to residencies is an invitation to zoom out from our human condition and to look at our work and our residencies as part of a wider living ecosystem. It is a call to build forms of ecological belonging which acknowledge our mutual interconnectedness with the more-than-human, moving at different pace and multiform rhythms of time.

But what does this mean in practice?

At the end of May 2021, I took part in a seminar at Zone2Source, an art space supporting work between the fields of art, nature, and technology, in a gorgeous old park in Amsterdam. Among many engaging conversations and group activities, there was also the invitation to partake in a soundwalk, *MycoMythology: Storytelling Circle* (2021), by Slovenian artist Saša Spačal. This work and the seminar were part of the launch of the School for MultiSpecies Knowledges, developed at Zone2Source by the curators Alice Smits and Irina Shapiro.

Equipped with my mobile phone and headphones, I went outside the gallery space in the surrounding area of the park together with the other seminar participants. A set of specific instructions spoken by a soothing voice accompanied our first movements. An initial reluctance (perhaps even a little embarrassment) towards following the suggested actions quickly vanished when we each started moving in different directions and lost sight of each other. The voice and sound created a sense of simultaneous intimacy and trust. It suddenly became easy to be totally embedded in oneself, and to look at the blades of grass, the small insects moving on the plants' leaves and the funny shapes of the branches of the old trees, and everything else around with different eyes.

We were all part of an "exercise in sensory attunement," where the known space quickly moved into an unknown one through carefully crafted instructions.[27]

27 Saša Spačal, MYCOMYTHOLOGIES STORYTELLING CIRCLE: HOW TO BE A MUSHROOM HUNTER SOUNDWALK, SoundCloud audio, 32:50, September 10, 2021. Available at: https://soundcloud.com/sa-a-spa-al/mycomythologies-storytelling-circle-how-to-be-a-mushroom-hunter-soundwalk?utm_source=clipboard&utm_medium=text&utm_campaign=social_sharing.

More information on the project are available here: https://www.agapea.si/en/projects/mycomythologies-storytelling-circle. Date accessed: 20 October 2021.

28 Ibid.

I remember distinctly two moments from this walk.

The first happened rather soon. I had reached a spot deep under a group of old trees and the voice invited me to dwell on it, on this threshold.

"Wherever this is for you, feel the
transition. Warm air at your back
from the interior of your house,
a building, your car, the subway,
and cool breeze on your face
from the outside world. Stand
there for a moment, and
really feel the in-between.
(...) To become a mushroom
hunter is to become a
master in the arts of
noticing.

To open into a deep
awareness of the
relationships that
surround you,
and employ
this awareness
as a tool of
attunement
to places,
objects,
or beings."[28]

While the voice
was describing the rich,
lively, and complex world
of mycelium under our feet, what
really struck me was the behaviour
of this network of fine white filaments,
particularly their capacity to move
in multiple directions at the same time.
As human beings, we can choose to
move only in one direction or another.

Left or right,

and eventually in succession,

one after

the

other

if we want more.

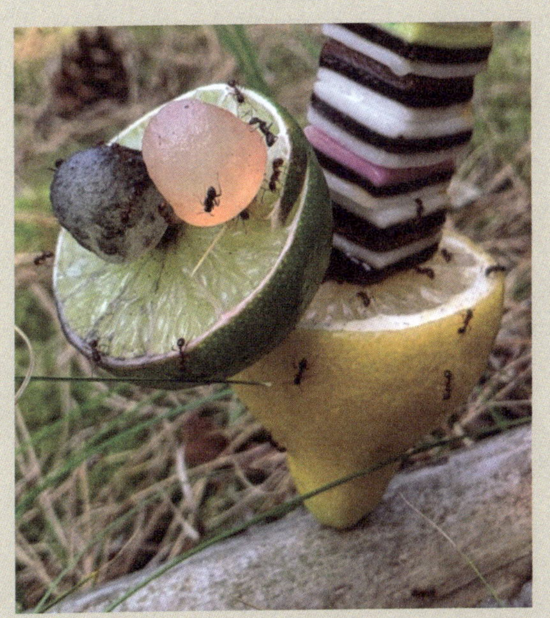

Documentation of the workshop "SCULPTURES FOR ANTS" (2019)
Organised by Semâ Bekirović and Jan-Pieter Karper at Into The Great Wide Open music festival.

In the case of mycelium, I learned:

> 'Mycelium are beings who have the power to choose both ways. Even more, they can choose all ways. When hyphae grow, they branch, like dendritic veins, from 1 to 2, to 4, to 8, to 16, to 32, to 64, and so on. And if they meet a threshold, their body can split themselves into multiples to explore both sides ... Once you are within this space, you may allow yourself to be mycelial and imagine yourself breaking apart, only to meet yourself again on some winding path."[29]

While standing in an isolated place and listening to this, I was mesmerised. I also remember feeling a bit jealous, thinking about this possibility.

29 Ibid.

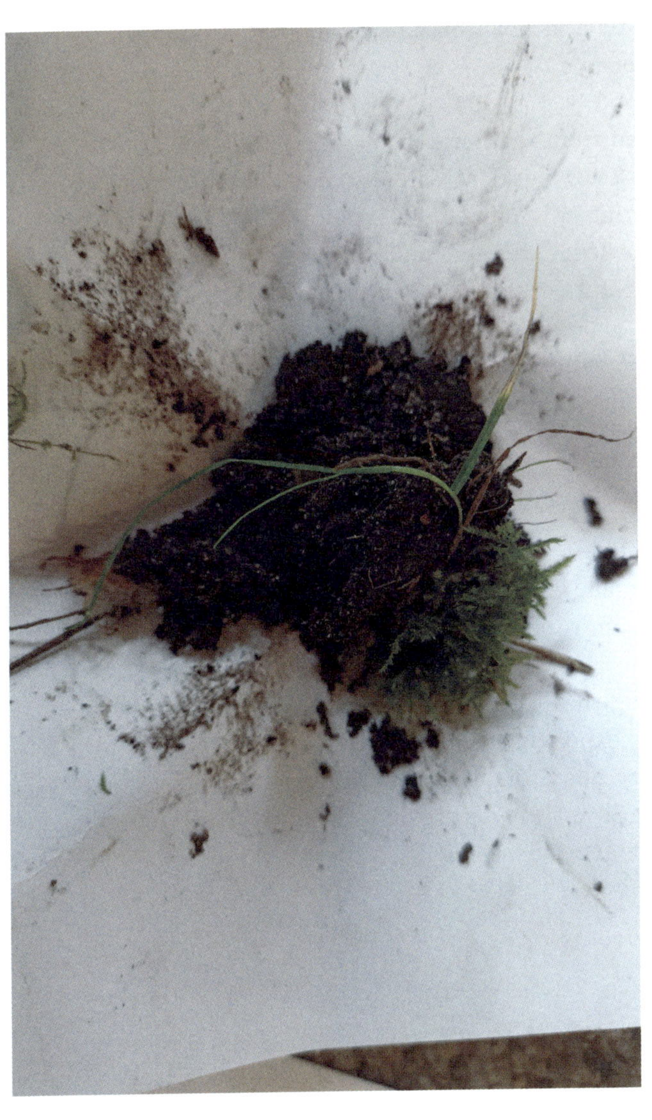

At the end
of the
soundwalk,
I crouched
down and
took a
handful of
dirt.

Upon
returning
to the
gallery, we
spent the
next hour
sharing
what had
happened.

There was a mutual sense of having had a powerful experience.

As I read from their statement, the School for Multi-Species Knowledges attempts to create an alternative un-learning environment to explore what kind of practices and knowledge can emerge from post-humanist and post-anthropocentric discourses.

> 'We will explore collaboratively learning tools and tactics that can help to attune ourselves differently to other life forms through understanding our codependencies."[30]

The School for MultiSpecies Knowledges has plans for a multi-annual practice-led exploration, which also includes an artist-in-residency programme in the park.[31]

Following the suggestions of Spačal's piece, and the physical experience I was part of, I wonder: How can we as residency operators attune to different rhythms around us, entering into truly deep connections with the environment around our residencies?

30 Open Call for the School for MultiSpecies Knowledges. (Email, 25 April 2022)

31 I also participated in the School for MultiSpecies Knowledges in 2022. Together with other participants, ranging from artists to designers, architects and researchers, I spent a six-week residency period using the Amstelpark as a test site for new ways to enter in relation with other multi-species. The main questions posed by the School were: What tactics do we need to tune into the rhythms of other life around us? What tools, vocabularies, practices, experiences and literacies appear when we start answering this question? And what kind of public formats can we develop to bring people along in our explorations?

During the residency I developed MESCOLANZA (2022), a set of cards and reading activities to connect words, places and species.

What's around us, where we work and our artists live and work, is made of different species, human and more than human.

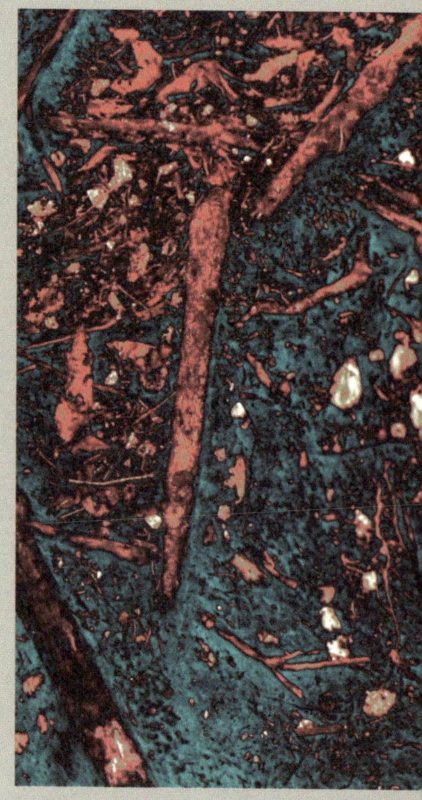

How can we take all of these into account?

They all have different rhythms and a different scale, from micro to the macro.

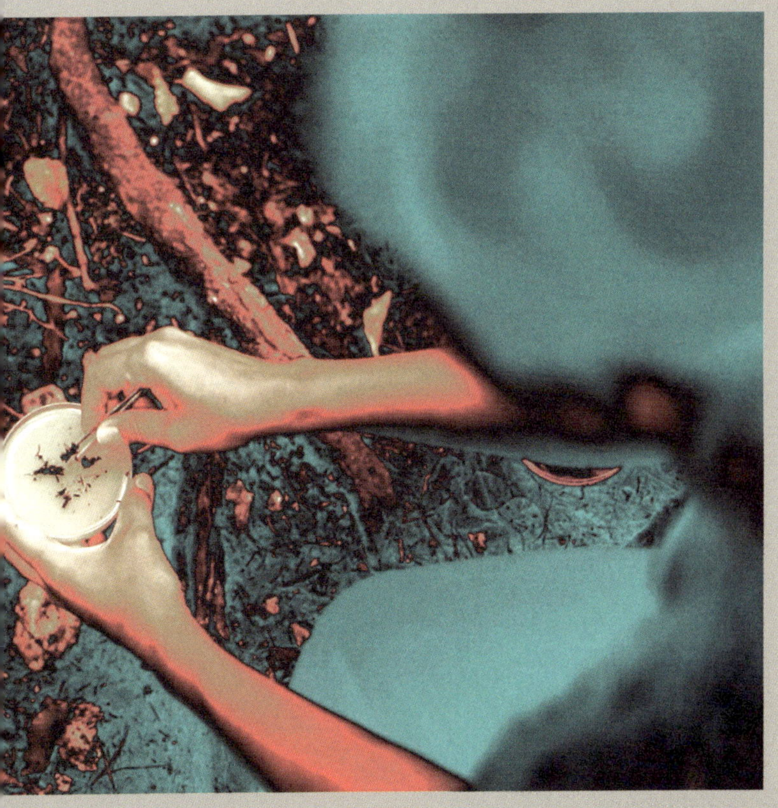

Saša Spačal, MYCOMYTHOLOGIES: RUPTURE (2020) — video still.
Courtesy of the artist

Perhaps, as the voice of Spačal's soundwalk suggested, taking another point of view, like that of the mycelium, can be of benefit to us. We can take many paths at once, growing further in directions that are more fruitful or simply more appealing — growing in relationship with all that surrounds us.

Thinking about these possibilities and their implications, Carlo Rovelli's engaging description about the non-existence of a single orderly sequence of times comes back to my mind.

As he explains, there is an absolute, organising temporal grammar distinguishing past, present, and future, but, in his view, this sequence is valid, only in relation to a specific space-time sequence.

> "The distinction between past, present and future is not an illusion. It is the temporal structure of the world. But the temporal structure of the world is not that of presentism."[32]

In philosophical terms presentism refers to the idea that only the present is real and that reality evolves from one present to a successive present.

32 Rovelli, THE ORDER OF TIME, 97

33 Ibid., 99

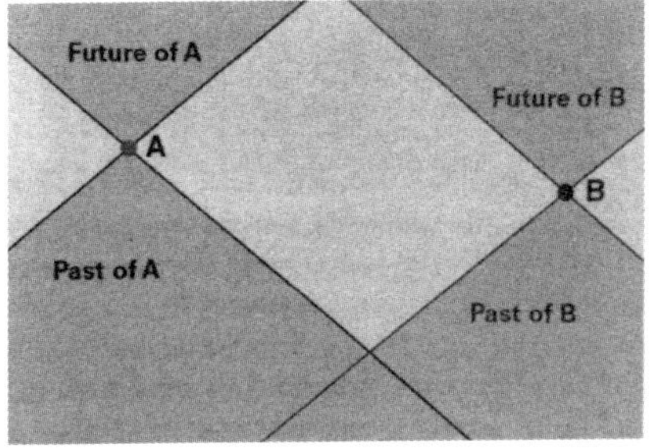

Rovelli's work shows that an objective global present does not exist, continuing:

> "We say that an event 'is,' or 'has been,' or 'will be.' We do not have a grammar adapted to say that an event 'has been' in relation to me but 'is' in relation to you. We must not be allowed to be confused by an inadequate grammar."[33]

I wonder, then, how we humans can actually attempt to move, so fluidly as the mycelium grows, among different directions abandoning a logic of mutual exclusion ("Or/Or", i.e. left or right) or unique timeline (a single type of past-present-future relation existing to describe what happens among all the different species that inhabit this world).

In order to try and attempt that,
I believe we should train other muscles.

Are we ready to train our imaginations, our smell, and our feet anew?

What would it mean to look at your residency through the tentacular body of the mycelium?

Imagine the fine filaments that are under the floor,

in the ground of your building.

Follow them.

What would you see?

What would you find?

Would you be embarrassed to share your findings with your colleagues?

If words are not enough, how would you translate what you just saw?

Or could you re-imagine the words we use now?

Puig de la Bellacasa reminds us that this relearning is not a nostalgic return to a pre-industrial landscape, nor is it a way to ignore pre-industrial unsustainable relations with soil. On the contrary, reconfiguring our human-soil relation is unique to a present that faces a global breakdown.

What are the new temporal imaginings we can create?

What are the rhythms of these different temporalities?

How can I break them or interfere with them?

Can I bring all these different temporalities and scales together, at least once?

As a way of a temporary conclusion,

I'd like to return
to the first image
I shared with you.

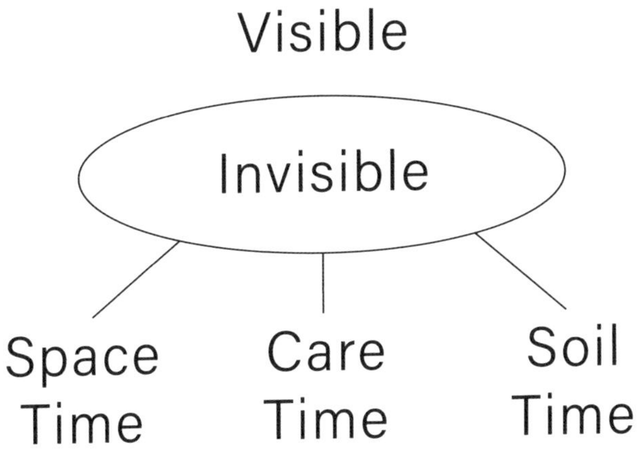

SPACE TIME

We can see that time in astrophysics or space time helps address what we do in a residency: the degrees of visibility of an artist's work and its different timelines of development. It pushes us to rethink how to engage differently with the residency period, thinking for instance of a time before and after it. It invites us to develop new ways to document the residency experience that are more in line with the needs stemming from the artistic practices and projects we are involved with, and less with the often standardised procedures of reports required by the funds.

CARE TIME

Care time is about how we do what we do. It touches on issues of office politics, life-work balance, as well as privileges linked to gender, race, and institutional roles. It asks us to rethink material and immaterial structures of work — from our habits to the infrastructures we use — and to be conscious of the values they express and are part of. It invites us to always be alert and mindful that our work is part of a larger social, political, and economic system that, unfortunately, tends to place care as an individual responsibility rather than a collective, political one.

Finally, soil time moves us to look at who with and for whom we do our work. To talk about ecosystems, multi-species, and different scales. It encourages us to think about an institutional ecosystem that respects everyone it comes into contact with. In order to do so, it invites us to explore our relationship with other organisms and to learn from the non-human elements with whom we live on this earth together.

Some of the examples mentioned in this text suggest ways and tools; others are incitements to question how time is used, described, and referred to in our work and that of the resident artists. I do not offer an exhaustive or recommended list of actions. I prefer to end this text with an invitation for you, dear reader, to use one section and some of the related questions to further think of conceptual or practical tools that you would like to use during your future residencies.

Which would you pick?

AFTERWORD

This essay is a revised version of a lecture given at the Summer Well symposium at the Saari Residence in Finland in 2021. Focused on residency research, this international assembly was curated by Irmeli Kokko and supported by the Kone Foundation. I am grateful to Irmeli Kokko for extending this invitation, as it enabled me to expand an earlier article and share it with a cohort of passionate and bright fellow researchers, some of whom have since become my dear companions in the Art Residency Research Collective (ARRC).

This work has evolved over time, following a spiral-like construction. Words and images from these pages have moved back and forth towards a central theme in a somewhat disharmonious way, mirroring the business of life. This centre to which I have always returned is a reflection on the experience of being "in residence," or curating one, in a present where the pressure to be productive and the continuous visibility are ever more out of sync with the rhythm of our minds, bodies, and the planet's resources.

Discussing different temporal perspectives within a residency is an invitation to seek ways through this unbalanced reality. It is an encouragement to reconfigure ways of working in a residency without being blind to the current socio-political context, and reproducing unhealthy or unsatisfactory processes.

In this pursuit, specific artworks have been fundamental in making my argument. While some of them were already present in the original text, others have come to find their place here from my digital archive in my laptop's folders. I'm indebted to each of these artists, as their works have offered me unending inspiration to develop the ideas in this book and something to hold onto whenever I was searching for the right words.

Lastly, I am very grateful to Cleo for bringing new life to this text through her vision, sensitivity and talent.

— Amsterdam, May 2024

This book is dedicated to my family, and all the people I love and make my time alive.

Angela Serino is a curator and researcher based in Amsterdam. She is an alumna of de Appel's Curatorial Programme and has a decade of experience working in artists residency programmes. She was the curator of RedLight Art Amsterdam (2009) for SMBA Stedelijk Museum Bureau and the City of Amsterdam; a member of the artistic committee of Kunsthuis SYB, a remote residency in Friesland (2010 – 2015); and curator-in-residence at several international institutions. She curated the "International Meeting of Residencies: Residencies as Learning Environments" (2015), promoted by AIR—artinresidence and FARE, in Milan, and edited the eponymous publication.
In 2020, she co-founded the Art Residency Research Collective (ARRC), which aims to study the shifting practices of art residencies through a hybrid residency format. More recently, she co-edited the academic journal *Between the Standing and the Inclined: Structures Supporting Change* (Kunstlicht Vol. 44 n.4, 2023).

IMAGES

Page 5
Toril Johannessen, *Historical Time*, 2011. Decimal clock, permanent installation at the University of Bergen. Courtesy of the artist.

Page 10 – 11
AiR Research map, 2016. Drawing printed on paper. Courtesy of the author and Marianna Maruyama. The map is composed of two layers. The first layer, in black, is *Notes on Residencies* (2015) by artist Marianna Maruyama, which was published in *Residencies as Learning Environments*. The map later expanded with an additional layer added during a working session I had with the artist at Kunsthuis SYB (22 – 27 March 2016).

Page 12
Book cover. Angela Serino (ed.), *Residencies as Learning Environments*, Milan: Fare (2015). Reprinted with kind permission of FARE.

Page 15
Book cover. Sarah Thelwall, *Size Matters: Notes towards a Better Understanding of the Value, Operation and Potential of Small Visual Arts Organisations*, London: Common Practice (2011). Reprinted with kind permission of Common Practice.

Page 19
Laura Wiedijk, *Waver*, 2012. Printed image. Courtesy of the artist.

Page 20 – 21
Laura Wiedijk, *Yield*, 2016. Video still. Courtesy of the artist.

Page 25
Book cover. Niko Doulos and Herbert Ploegman (eds.), *Unpacking Residencies: Situating the Production of Cultural Relations,* Kunstlicht, Vol. 39, n.2 (2018). Reprinted with kind permission of Kunstlicht.

Page 31
Photograph by the author.

Page 35 – 39
Louise Bourgeois, *The Insomnia Drawings*, 1994 – 1995. Three of 220 mixed media works on paper of varying dimensions. Detail shown here: ink and pencil on music paper, 30.5 × 22 cm. Photo: Christopher Burke, © The Easton Foundation/ Licensed by Pictoright, NL and VAGA at Artists Rights Society (ARS), NY

Page 40
Carlo Rovelli, *The Order of Time*, New York: Riverhead Books (2018), 94. Drawings. Courtesy of the author.

Page 41
Carlo Rovelli, *The Order of Time*, New York: Riverhead Books (2018), 47, 109. Drawings. Courtesy of the author.

Page 46 – 47
Book cover. Lívia Páldi (ed.), *The Site Residency*, Berlin: BAC — Baltic Art Center and Sternberg Press (2017). Design: Krzysztof Pyda. Reprinted with kind permission of Lívia Páldi and Sternberg Press.

Page 50 – 51
Every Ocean Hughes, *Beyond the will to measure*, 2014. Ceramic clocks, variable dimensions up to 14 m. Photo: Doryun Kim. Courtesy of the artist.

Page 55
Photograph by the author.

Page 58 – 59
Katja Mater, *Time is an Arrow, Error 02*, 2020. Two C-prints. Courtesy of the artist and LambdaLambdaLambda Prishtina/Paris.

Page 64
Book cover. Miriam Wistreich, Josine Sibum Siderius and Heidi Vogels (eds.), *On Affecting Change Through Artist-in-Residencies*, Hotel Maria Kapel, Kunsthuis SYB, DutchCulture | TransArtists: Amsterdam (2021).

Reprinted with kind permission of Hotel Maria Kapel, Kunsthuis SYB, DutchCulture | TransArtists.

Page 65
Maja Bekan, Griet Menschaert, Miriam Wistreich, *Slow Burn*, 2019. Space intervention.
Courtesy of Hotel Maria Kapel.

Page 66 – 67
Harriet Rose Morley, *Tools for Collective Navigation*, 2020. Still from screensaver rendered by Alex Paul Burch. Courtesy of the artist and Alex Paul Burch.

Page 68
Book cover. *Unlearning Exercises: Art Organizations as Sites for Unlearning*, Utrecht, The Netherlands: Casco Art Institute, Working for the Commons; Amsterdam: Valiz (2018). Editors: Binna Choi, Annette Krauss, Yolande van der Heide, Liz Allan. Contributors: Liz Allan, Yollotl Alvarado, Antariksa, Jacob Apostol, Binna Choi, Joy Melanie Escani, Andrés García, Brigitta Isabella, Faisol Iskandor, Ismiatun, Nancy Jouwe, Annette Krauss, Emily Pethick, Andrea Phillips, Ying Que, Kerstin Stakemeier, Sakiko Sugawa, Syafiatudina, Ferdiansyah Thajib, Marina Vishmidt, Yolande van der Heide, Erminah Zaenah, and the shifting team at Casco Art Institute: Working for the Commons.
Design: Rosen Eveleigh.
Courtesy of the authors.

Page 70
Unlearning Exercises: Art Organizations as Sites for Unlearning, 20 – 21.Images from the e-book. Courtesy of the authors.

Page 72 – 73
Unlearning Exercises: Art Organizations as Sites for Unlearning, 28 – 29. Images from the ebook. Courtesy of the authors.

Page 75
Tamara Kuselman, work-in-progress of *A Pool Without a Rim*, 2020.
Courtesy of the artist.

Page 78 – 80
School of Temporalities (Maja Bekan, Annette Krauss, and Julia Wieger), *How Is Public Time?*, 2021. Posters.
Courtesy of the artists.

Page 84
Photograph by the author.

Page 91
Documentation of the workshop *"Sculptures for Ants"* (2019), organised by Semâ Bekirović and Jan-Pieter Karper at Into The Great Wide Open music festival. Courtesy of Semâ Bekirović and Jan-Pieter Karper.

Page 93
A handful of earth collected in Amstelpark during the soundwalk, *MycoMythologies Storytelling Circle: How To Be A Mushroom Hunter Soundwalk* (2021), by Saša Spačal.
Photograph by the author.

Page 96 – 97
Saša Spačal, *MycoMythologies: Rupture*, 2020. Video still.
Courtesy of the artist.

Page 99
Carlo Rovelli, *The Order of Time*, New York: Riverhead Books (2018), 45.
Drawing. Courtesy of the author.

Set Margins' #41

Configurations of Time:
Imagining Other Temporalities
in the Artist Residency
by Angela Serino

ISBN: 978-90-834041-9-6

Editor: Angela Serino
Book Design: Cleo Tsw
Copyeditor: Olamiju Fajemisin
Advisor: Freek Lomme

Printer: Printon, Estonia
Edition: 1500 copies

Fonts: CMU Serif, Acumin

Earlier versions of some chapters of this book have appeared in article form. An extended version of Chapter 1 ("Space Time") appeared as "Cultivating Time" in Niko Doulos and Herbert Ploegman (eds.), *Unpacking Residencies: Situating the Production of Cultural Relations*, Kunstlicht, Vol. 39, No. 2 (2018), 60 – 73. Part of Chapter 2 ("Care Time") appeared as "A Shock Can Be Many Things. A Shock Can Bring Many Things" in *Station to Station #4 Game Changer*, DutchCulture | TransArtists, Amsterdam (2022), 22 – 29.

Made possible thanks to
Mondriaan Foundation, Angela Serino,
and Freek Lomme.

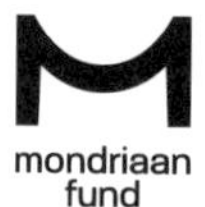

With thanks to the artists and authors for their inspiration and for generously granting permission to use images of their work:
Semâ Bekirović and Jan-Pieter Karper
Louise Bourgeois — The Easton Foundation
Casco Art Institute: Working for the Commons, and the contributors of *Unlearning Exercises*
DutchCulture | TransArtists
Every Ocean Hughes
Hotel Maria Kapel
Toril Johannessen
Annette Krauss
Kunsthuis SYB
Tamara Kuselman
Marianna Maruyama
Katja Mater
Harriet Rose Morley
Lívia Páldi
Carlo Rovelli
School of Temporalities (Annette Krauss, Julia Wieger, Maja Bekan)
Saša Spačal
Laura Wiedijk

Special thanks to:
Patricia Healy McMeans, Giuseppe Greco, Vesna Madzoski, Rumiko Hagiwara, Melanja Palitta, Maja Bekan, ARRC (Pau Catà, Morag Iles, Miriam La Rosa, Patricia Healy McMeans), Irmeli Kokko

First Edition. 2024.

Set Margins'

www.setmargins.press